ESSENTIAL
DUBLIN

★ Best places to see 34–55

■ Featured sight

Original text by Hilary Weston and Jackie Staddon
Updated by Apostrophe S

© Automobile Association Developments Limited 2009
First published 2007
Reprinted 2009. Information verified and updated

ISBN: 978-0-7495-6009-6

Published by AA Publishing, a trading name of Automobile Association Developments
Limited, whose registered office is Fanum House, Basing View, Basingstoke,
Hampshire RG21 4EA. Registered number 1878835.

Colour separation: MRM Graphics Ltd
Printed and bound in Italy by Printer Trento S.r.l.

A03616
Maps in this title based on Ordnance Survey Ireland. Permit No. 8430
© Ordnance Survey Ireland and Government of Ireland
Transport map © Communicarta Ltd, UK

About this book

Symbols are used to denote the following categories:

- ✚ map reference to maps on cover
- ✉ address or location
- ☎ telephone number
- 🕐 opening times
- 💷 admission charge
- 🍴 restaurant or café on premises or nearby
- Ⓜ nearest underground train station
- 🚌 nearest bus/tram route
- 🚉 nearest overground train station
- ⛴ nearest ferry stop
- ✈ nearest airport
- ❓ other practical information
- ℹ tourist information
- ▶ indicates the page where you will find a fuller description

This book is divided into six sections.

The essence of Dublin pages 6–19
Introduction; Features; Food and drink; Short break including the 10 Essentials

Planning pages 20–33
Before you go; Getting there; Getting around; Being there

Best places to see pages 34–55
The unmissable highlights of any visit to Dublin

Best things to do pages 56–77
Great pubs; stunning views, places to take the children and more

Exploring pages 78–155
The best places to visit in Dublin, organized by area

Excursions pages 156–183
Places to visit out of town

Maps

All map references are to the maps on the covers. For example, Temple Bar has the reference ✚ 21J – indicating the grid square in which it is to be found.

Admission prices

Inexpensive (under €3)
Moderate (€3–€6)
Expensive (over €6)

Hotel prices

Price are per room per night:
€ budget (under €100);
€€ moderate (€100–€200);
€€€ expensive to luxury (over €200)

Restaurant prices

Price for a three-course meal per person without drinks:
€ budget (under €25);
€€ moderate (€25–€45);
€€€ expensive (over €45)

Contents

The essence of...

Dublin offers everything you would expect from a
capital city – elegant architecture, superb museums,
vibrant cultural life, great restaurants – and it is a
fantastic place to party. Its close proximity to lush
green mountains and coastal towns adds to the appeal.
In a city that has suffered a turbulent and often
oppressed past, Dubliners have retained a strong sense
of pride and identity that, together with their charming
and witty character, makes them impossible to resist.
With a booming economy and growing immigrant
population, more restaurants and trendy bars are
opening up alongside the many traditional pubs. Without doubt, Dublin is having fun and the *craic* (Irish for
fun) is flowing. Give it a try; you won't be disappointed.

features

In Dublin it can rain non-stop for days, with howling gales that can blow umbrellas inside out, but even when the outlook is grey there is something very special and unique about this city, much of it because of the people, who are laid back, with a great sense of humour and exceptional conversational skills. There is also a sense of intimacy about the city itself. It takes only a few days of strolling around to get to know the place, and Dubliners still bump into people they know on the street – little chance of that happening in London or Paris.

But Dublin has a split personality, on one side striving to be cosmopolitan, on the other still rough around the edges. It can be calm and soothing or lively and exhilarating; chic and modern with trendy bars and young high-flyers, or old-fashioned with traditional pubs and an older generation still hanging on to pre-EU values. With a booming economy, Dublin is changing, but as the surge of partying visitors and sophisticated bars and restaurants continue to shape the city, old Dublin is still – for now – holding its ground.

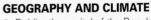

GEOGRAPHY AND CLIMATE

● Dublin, the capital of the Republic of Ireland, is on the Irish Sea at the mouth of the River Liffey, and covers an area of 115sq km (44sq miles).

● Greater Dublin's limits are Howth to the north and Bray Head to the south.

● There are three main waterways running through the city: the River Liffey, and the Royal and Grand canals. All offer pleasant waterside walks.

● Just south of the city are the Wicklow Mountains; their highest point, Lugnaquilla, is 926m (3,038ft).

● Dublin is the driest area of Ireland, with a maximum annual rainfall of 750mm (30in), and has mild winters and cool summers.

ARCHITECTURE

● Dublin is famous for its Georgian architecture, best seen in Merrion Square and Fitzwilliam Square. Much is made of the doorways of the buildings here, featuring on countless posters and postcards.

POPULATION

● The population of Greater Dublin is just over 1.6 million; the total population of the Republic of Ireland is 4.2 million. More than 40 per cent of people in the Republic live within 90km (56 miles) of Dublin.

● Approximately 39 per cent of the population is under 25.

food & drink

The choice of places to eat out in Dublin is excellent and the standard of many restaurants is first class. There is a strong emphasis on global cuisine, with options as diverse as Mongolian, Lebanese, Mexican and Nepalese. A host of talented Irish chefs is now on the scene, ensuring good standards and the use of local ingredients.

Traditional Irish cuisine and good pub grub have enjoyed a revival, with the occasional international influence. Irish seafood is legendary, particularly fresh oysters, fresh and smoked salmon and the well-known Dublin Bay prawns. Generally restaurants are not cheap, but there are some good-value set meals available.

IRISH CUISINE

Irish cooking has a reputation for being plain but plentiful, which is far from true – traditional dishes consist of wonderfully rich flavours and interesting taste combinations. The best chefs have moved away from the heavier dishes, which were mostly served to hard-working farmers and fishermen, and have created a new Irish cuisine, a fusion of flavours to produce a lighter result, but still reflecting the traditional theme. Some long-established choices remain, such as Dublin coddle (a sausage stew), but an alternative is to make it with

shellfish, producing a lighter meal. Irish stew is still popular, as are potato dishes such as champ (mashed with chives and butter) or colcannon (mashed and mixed with leek, butter, cabbage, cream and nutmeg), which are served as a tasty accompaniment. Boxties (potato pancakes with various savoury fillings) are served as a main course.

Irish bread is not just something to make a sandwich with. There are many tasty varieties that need only a spreading of butter or are used as a side dish for home-made soup. Soda bread, or wheaten bread, made with stone-ground flour, has a wonderful flavour and texture, then there are the fruity tea breads such as barm brack.

There is even a potato bread (mashed potato mixed with flour and egg) that is cooked on a griddle and usually served with the hearty traditional Irish breakfast of bacon, eggs, sausage and black (or white) pudding – another type of sausage.

WHAT TO DRINK?

Think of Irish beer and Guinness springs to mind; it's been brewed in Dublin since 1799. Sold in at least 30 countries worldwide, it is an enduring symbol of Irishness, but undoubtedly tastes best on Irish soil, with its cool, biting flavour and thick creamy head. Lager is also widely available to those who prefer a lighter drink.

Irish whiskey has a wonderful clean taste, quite different from Scotch whisky or American bourbon. There are no longer any whiskey distilleries in Dublin, although Jameson's is still a household name; it was distilled in the city up until 1971.

short break

If you have only a short time to visit Dublin and would like to take home some unforgettable memories, you can do something local and capture the real flavour of the city. The following suggestions will give you a wide range of sights and experiences that won't take long, won't cost very much and will make your visit very special.

● **Soak up the atmosphere in Temple Bar** (➤ 91) over a pint, a glass of wine or a cappuccino, or just watch the street entertainers in the square.

● **Drink a pint of Guinness at the top of the Guinness Storehouse** (➤ 42–43) in the Gravity Bar. The view is breathtaking and the pint comes free with your ticket, a great culmination to the fascinating story of brewing the 'black stuff'.

● **Window-shop on Grafton Street, with a coffee at Bewley's** (➤ 105) – Dublin's most famous tea room in the chic end of town.

● **Walk the Liffey Quays** along the north-side boardwalk for great views of the river and some of the best examples of grand Georgian buildings.

THE ESSENCE OF DUBLIN

- **Enjoy a music session** and a bit of *craic* in the pub and you'll soon realize how important tradition is to Dubliners.

- **Visit Kilmainham Gaol** (➤ 46–47) to learn about the struggle for Irish independence and appreciate what life was like for the prisoners.

- **Take a guided literary walk or a ghost tour** (➤ 64) to see the less obvious side of the city. Try the literary or musical pub crawl, or the Dublin Ghostbus for a chilling experience.

- **Buy a Dublin Pass**, the best way to see all the main attractions at a reduced rate. Contact the tourist office for the 1-, 2-, 3- or 6-day passes.

- **Ride the DART** both north and south along Dublin Bay. In minutes you are out of the city and rattling alongside the coast.

- **Stroll around the Georgian district** to view the doorways painted in a variety of colours and topped by picturesque fanlights and wrought iron balconies above.

Planning

Before you go

WHEN TO GO

JAN	FEB	MAR	APR	MAY	JUN	JUL	AUG	SEP	OCT	NOV	DEC
8°C	8°C	10°C	13°C	15°C	18°C	20°C	19°C	17°C	14°C	10°C	8°C
46°F	46°F	50°F	55°F	59°F	64°F	68°F	66°F	63°F	57°F	50°F	46°F

🌧 High season 🌫 Low season

Temperatures are the average daily maximum for each month.

The best time to visit Dublin is between April and October, when the weather is at its best, although the city is very popular at any time of the year.

The peak tourist months are July and August; reserve accommodation early. Christmas and the New Year are also popular. During November to March, the weather can be changeable. Most of the time it is cloudy, and frequently wet, dark and dreary. Autumn is generally fine, with a high percentage of crisp days and clear skies. Be prepared for rain at some time during your stay, no matter when you visit, but try to accept the rain as the Irish do – as a 'wet blessing'.

WHAT YOU NEED

● Required
○ Suggested
▲ Not required

Some countries require a passport to remain valid for a minimum period (usually at least six months) beyond the date of entry – contact their consulate or embassy or your travel agent for details.

	UK	Germany	USA	Netherlands	Spain
Passport (or National Identity Card where applicable)					
Visa (regulations can change – check before you travel)	▲	▲	▲	▲	▲
Onward or Return Ticket	▲	▲	▲	▲	▲
Health Inoculations (tetanus and polio)	▲	▲	▲	▲	▲
Health Documentation (➤ 23, Health insurance)	●	●	●	●	▲
Travel Insurance	○	○	○	○	○
Driving Licence (national)	●	●	●	●	●
Car Insurance Certificate	●	●	●	●	●
Car Registration Document	●	●	●	●	●

WEBSITES

www.visitdublin.com
www.dublin.ie

www.dublintourist.com
www.discoverireland.com

TOURIST OFFICES AT HOME

In the UK

Tourism Ireland
✉ 103 Wigmore Street, London,
W1U 1QS
☎ 0207 513 0880

In the USA

Tourism Ireland
✉ 345 Park Avenue, New York,
NY 10154
☎ 212/418 0800
www.tourismireland.com

In Australia

Tourism Ireland
✉ 5th Level, 36 Carrington Street,
Sydney, NSW 2000
☎ 02 9299 6177

HEALTH INSURANCE

Nationals of EU and countries with which Ireland has a reciprocal agreement can get medical treatment at reduced cost in Ireland with an EHIC (European Health Insurance Card, not required for UK nationals), although private medical insurance is still advised and is essential for all other visitors.

This also applies to dental treatment within the Irish health service on production of an EHIC (not needed for UK nationals).

TIME DIFFERENCES

GMT 12 noon	Ireland 12 noon	Germany 1PM	USA (NY) 7AM	Netherlands 1PM	Spain 1PM

Ireland observes Greenwich Mean Time (GMT), but from late March, when clocks are put forward one hour, until late October, summer-time (GMT +1) operates.

NATIONAL HOLIDAYS

1 January *New Year's Day*
17 March *St Patrick's Day*
March/April *Good Friday*
March/April
Easter Monday
May (1st Mon)
May Holiday
June (1st Mon)
June Holiday

August (1st Mon)
August Holiday
October (last Mon)
All Soul's Day
25 December
Christmas Day
26 December
St Stephen's Day

Most shops, offices and museums close on these days. Good Friday is not a public holiday in the Republic, but many businesses observe it, so expect to find some offices, restaurants and pubs closed on this day.

WHAT'S ON WHEN

January *New Year's Day Parade:* Marching bands from all over the world come together in Dublin for the parade.

February *International Film Festival:* The best Irish and international cinema is shown over a period of two weeks at this increasingly popular festival.

March *St Patrick's Day:* A popular date in Dublin's calendar, celebrated by a week of street entertainment, concerts, exhibitions and fireworks, building up to a huge parade on the day itself (17 March), usually starting near St Patrick's Cathedral.

May *Heineken Green Energy Music Festival:* Staged over the May bank holiday weekend, this major festival has featured top international stars since it began in the mid-1990s. There is normally an open-air concert in the grounds of Dublin Castle.

June *Bloomsday:* On 16 June each year, the day James Joyce set his novel *Ulysses*, Joycean fans celebrate the man and his works with tours, readings and seminars.

July *Dublin Jazz Festival:* A live, five-day schedule of music performed by artists from around the world. In Temple Bar and other locations.

Dublin Pride: The gay and lesbian scene is flourishing in Dublin, and this month-long festival is celebrated in a big way. It includes a free open-air show at the Civic Offices. (Sometimes held in June.)

August *Dublin Horse Show:* The best show horses and show jumpers descend on the RDS grounds in the first week of August for Ireland's equine highlight of the year.

Liffey Swim: This has been a Dublin institution since 1924 – 400 or so people dive into the River Liffey in the centre of Dublin for a race through 2km (1.2 miles) of murky waters, while spectators line the bridges to watch. (Sometimes held in September.)

September *Dublin Theatre Festival:* A two-week festival, among the most vibrant in Europe, attracting all the leading names from Dublin's drama scene. The many venues include the Abbey and the Gate theatres.

October *Dublin City Marathon:* On the last Monday in October thousands of enthusiastic runners turn out for the 42km (26-mile) run through the streets of Dublin.

Samhain: An evening parade and fireworks for Dublin's Hallowe'en festival, based on the pagan festival of Samhain in celebration of the dead and the end of the Celtic summer.

December *Christmas National Hunt Festival:* A major four-day race meeting at Leopardstown racecourse.

Getting there

BY AIR

Dublin Airport

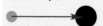

11km (7 miles) to city centre

 30 minutes

 20 minutes

Regular flights operate from Britain, mainland Europe and North America. The national airline is Aer Lingus (tel: 844 4747; www.aerlingus.ie). Ryanair (tel: 844 4411; www.ryanair.com) offers low-cost flights. Dublin Airport is 11km (7 miles) from the centre, journey time 30 minutes by bus or 20 minutes by taxi.

To get to Dublin city centre by car, take the M1 south. The journey takes between 20 minutes and an hour, depending on traffic.

Taxis are always metered and a journey to the city centre should cost around €20.

There are several bus options to reach Dublin city centre. Airlink: No 747 leaves every quarter hour for O'Connell Street, Busáras (the central bus terminal) and Parnell Square; No 748 also goes to Tara Street, Aston Quay and Heuston Station. Tickets are available at the CIE Information Desk in Arrivals. For information, contact Dublin Bus (tel: 873 4222; www.dublinbus.ie). Aircoach express: operates 5am–midnight, with departures every 15 minutes for city-centre stops including O'Connell Street, Grafton Street, Merrion Square North, Pembroke Road and St Stephen's Green; get tickets from the Tourist Information desk in Arrivals.

Contact Aircoach (tel: 844 7118; www.aircoach.ie) for information. The cheapest way into the city is by public bus (Nos 16A, 41, 41B and 747), but they are slower than Airlink and Aircoach services because they make many stops along the way; buses leave every 10–20 minutes for Eden Quay, near O'Connell Street.

BY SEA

Ferries from the UK sail into the ports of
Dublin, 5km (3 miles) east of the city, and
Dun Laoghaire (pronounced 'Dunleary'),
14km (9 miles) south of the city.

If travelling by car, simply follow
city-centre signs.

Taxis operate from both ports into the
centre of Dublin, with a journey time of
around 20 minutes.

There's an inexpensive DART service (► 28) from Dun Laoghaire to
Dublin, running half-hourly (sometimes more often) to Pearse, Tara Street
and Connolly stations in the city centre. The journey takes 25 minutes.

Public buses run regularly: Nos 7, 7A, 46A or 46X from Dun Laoghaire
DART Station; Nos 53 or 53A from Dublin Port. Dublin Bus operates a
shuttle service to Busáras (the central bus station) every half-hour
7am–11:10pm. The journey takes around 30 minutes.

BY TRAIN

Dublin has two mainline stations: Connolly serves the north, Heuston
serves the south and west of Ireland. Buses and taxis are available at both
stations. For rail information, contact Irish Rail/Iarnród Éireann (tel: 836
6222; www.irishrail.ie).

BY ROAD

The main motorway routes into the city are the M1 from Belfast and the
north, and the M11/N11 from Wicklow and the south. The ring road M50
skirts around the city with several roads leading off into central Dublin. The
N31 leads from the ferry port of Dun Laoghaire onto the N11 and directly
into the centre.

Congestion has been a big problem in Dublin in recent years, but with
the building of the Port Tunnel, which opened in December 2006, more
lorries from the port have been diverted away from the city and directly
onto the motorways.

Parking in the city is not easy – fines for illegal parking are severe – but
most hotels and guest houses have parking available for guests.

For driving in Dublin ► 29.

Getting around

PUBLIC TRANSPORT

Internal flights Flights from Dublin to other airports in Ireland are operated by Aer Lingus (➤ 26) and Aer Arann (tel: 814 1058; www.aerarann.ie).

Trains Ireland has a limited network run by Iarnród Éireann (tel: 703 2358; www.irishrail.ie), which serves major towns and cities. Dublin has two main stations; trains from the north arrive at Connolly Station and trains from the south and west arrive at Heuston Station.

Long-distance buses Bus Éireann (tel: 836 6111; www.buseireann.ie) operates a network of express bus routes out of Dublin serving most of the country (some run during summer months only).

Urban transport The city's extensive bus service is run by Dublin Bus (59 Upper O'Connell Street; tel: 873 4222; www.dublinbus.ie). As there are so many different buses that run across the city, Dublin Bus provides free individual timetables for each route. The Rapid Transit system (DART) runs along the coast from Malahide in the north to Greystones in the south (tel: 836 6222; www.irishrail.ie/dart). The Luas light railway operates from the centre out to the suburbs. A range of fare-saving combined travel passes is available.

TAXIS

Taxi stands are outside hotels, train and bus stations, and at major locations such as St Stephen's Green, Dame Street, O'Connell Street and Dawson Street. Taxis can be hailed on the street but late at night they can be in short supply so you might have to wait in line.

National Radio Cabs ☎ 708 9292   City Cabs ☎ 872 7272

FARES AND CONCESSIONS

Students under 18 are entitled to reduced entrance in some museums and galleries. Be sure to carry some form of identification. Holders of an International Student Identity Card can buy a Travelsave Stamp entitling them to travel discounts, including a 20 per cent reduction on Bus Éireann, Iarnród Éireann and Irish Ferries (between Britain and Ireland). Contact your local student travel agency for further details. The Travelsave Stamp can be purchased from USIT (19 Aston Quay, Dublin 2; tel: 602 1777; www.usit.ie).

Senior citizens (over 60) are entitled to discounts on transport and most admission fees, on proof of age.

DRIVING

- Drive on the left.
- Speed limit on motorways: 112kph/70mph; dual carriageways: 96kph/60mph. Speed limit on country roads: 96kph/60mph. Speed limit on urban roads: 48kph/30mph (or as signposted).
- Seatbelts must be worn in front seats at all times and in rear seats where fitted.
- Random breath-testing takes places. Never drive under the influence of alcohol.
- Lead replacement petrol (LRP) and unleaded petrol are widely available. Many fuel stations in and around Dublin stay open 24 hours, while those in the villages and more rural areas stay open until 8 or 9pm, and open after Mass on Sundays.
- If your your own car breaks down and you are a member of an AIT-affiliated motoring club, you can call the Automobile Association's rescue service (tel: 1800 667788). If the car is rented follow the instructions given in the documentation; most of the international rental firms provide a rescue service.

CAR RENTAL

Car rental in Dublin is expensive. All of the main international car rental companies are represented; however, a car from a local company is likely to be cheaper, but may not allow different pick-up/drop-off points. For July and August it is best to make reservations well ahead.

Being there

TOURIST OFFICES

Fáilte Ireland, Baggot Street Bridge, Baggot Street, Dublin 2 ☎ 602 4000;
www.failteireland.ie

Dublin Tourism, St Andrew's Church, Suffolk Street, Dublin 2 ☎ 605 7700;
www.visitdublin.com

Walk-in centres
14 Upper O'Connell Street, Dublin Airport, Dun Laoghaire ferry terminal, The Square, Tallaght (southern suburbs)

Discover Ireland East Coast
Dublin Road, Mullingar, Co Westmeath ☎ 044 48650;
www.discoverireland.ie/eastcoast

MONEY

The euro (€) is the official currency of the Republic of Ireland, which is divided into 100 cents. Coins come in denominations of 1, 2, 5, 10, 20 and 50 cents, €1 and 2, and notes come in €5, 10, 20, 50, 100, 200 and 500 denominations (the last two are rarely seen). The notes and one side of the coins are the same throughout the European single currency zone, but each country has a different design on one face of each of the coins.

POSTAL AND INTERNET SERVICES

The main post office, in O'Connell Street, opens Mon–Sat 8–8; hours for other post offices are generally Mon–Fri 9–5:30, Sat 9–1. Post-boxes are green; stamps are sold at post offices, some newsagents or are available from machines.

TIPS AND GRATUITIES

Yes ✓ No ✗		
Restaurants (if service not included)	✓	10%
Cafés/bars (if service not included)	✓	10%
Taxis	✓	10%
Porters	✓	€2
Tour guides	✓	€2
Toilets	✗	

Many hotels offer internet services or WiFi connections. There are also an increasing number of internet cafés such as Global Internet Café at 8 Lower O'Connell Street (tel: 878 0295; www.globalcafe.ie; open: Mon–Fri 8am–11pm, Sat 9am–11pm, Sun 10am–11pm) and Central Cybercafé at 6 Grafton Street (tel: 677 8298; www.globalcafe.ie; open: Mon–Fri 9am–10pm, Sat–Sun 10–9). Rates vary according to time of day, but are lower before noon and after 8pm.

TELEPHONES
Public telephone boxes are blue and cream or the glass-booth style, and take coins or phone cards (sold at post offices and newsagents). The Dublin code is 01; dial 10 for national operator assistance and 114 for the international operator. All numbers preceded with 1800 are toll-free.

International dialling codes
From Ireland to:
UK: 00 44
USA: 00 1
Germany: 00 49
Netherlands: 00 31
Spain: 00 34
Australia: 00 61

Emergency telephone numbers
Police: 999
Fire: 999
Ambulance: 999
Coastal Rescue: 999

EMBASSIES AND CONSULATES
UK ☎ 205 3700
Germany ☎ 269 3011
USA ☎ 668 8777

Netherlands ☎ 269 3444
Spain ☎ 260 8066

HEALTH ADVICE
Sun advice The sunniest months are June and July with on average 5–6.5 hours of sun a day, though July and August are the hottest. During these months you should take precautions – cover up, use a good sunscreen and drink plenty of water.

Drugs Prescription and non-prescription drugs and medicines are available from pharmacies. When closed, most pharmacies display details of the nearest one that is open. In an emergency, contact a hospital.

Safe water Tap water in Ireland is perfectly safe to drink. However, if you prefer to drink bottled water you will find it widely available, though it is often expensive, particularly in restaurants.

PERSONAL SAFETY

Street crime was rare in Dublin, but now petty crime is increasing.

- Keep valuables in your hotel safe.
- Pickpockets and bag snatching are prevalent.
- Watch handbags and wallets in public places.
- Avoid Phoenix Park and poorly lit alleys and side-streets after dark.
- Keep cars secured and property out of view.

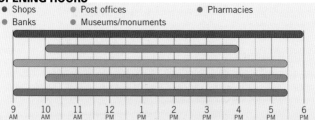

The national police, called the Garda Síochána (pronounced shee-kaw-nah), wear blue uniforms and, in bad weather, yellow raincoats.

Police assistance:
☎ 999 from any call box

ELECTRICITY

The power supply is 240 volts AC. Sockets are usually the UK type, with three square pins. Parts of the Republic also have two round pins (Continental type).

Overseas visitors should bring a voltage transformer and plug adaptor.

OPENING HOURS

- Shops
- Post offices
- Pharmacies
- Banks
- Museums/monuments

| 9 AM | 10 AM | 11 AM | 12 PM | 1 PM | 2 PM | 3 PM | 4 PM | 5 PM | 6 PM |

In addition to times shown above, some shops open on Sunday. Late-night shopping is on Thursday, with many places open until 8pm. Most banks close on Saturdays; some remain open till 5pm on Thursdays. City-centre post offices open on Saturday mornings. Pharmacies display a list of pharmacies that open at night and on Sundays.

Museum hours vary according to the season, so always check ahead.

LANGUAGE

Irish is a Celtic language, probably introduced to Ireland by the Celts in the last few centuries BC. Ireland has two official languages, English and Irish, but everyone speaks English, although you may hear Irish in the Gaeltacht areas of the west and south. You will come across Irish on road signs, buses and trains. Below is a list of some words that you may see while in Ireland, with a guide to pronunciation.

yes	*tá/sea*	hello	*dia dhuit*
no	*níl/ní hea*	goodbye	*slán*
please	*le do thoil*	goodnight	*oíche mhaith*
thank you	*go raibh maith agat*	how much?	*cé mhéid?*
welcome	*fáilte*	open/closed	*oscailte/dúnta*
hotel	*óstán*	double room	*seomra dúbailte*
bed and breakfast	*loístín oíche*	chambermaid	*cailín aimsire*
single room	*seomra singil*	room service	*seirbhís seomraí*
bank	*an banc*	coin	*bonn*
exchange office	*oifig malairte*	travellers' cheque	*seic taistil*
post office	*oifig an phoist*	credit card	*cárta creidmheasa*
restaurant	*bialann*	breakfast	*bricfeásta*
café	*caife*	lunch	*lón*
pub/bar	*tábhairne*	dinner	*dinnéar*
aeroplane	*eitleán*	station	*stáisiún*
airport	*aerfort*	boat	*bád*
train	*traein*	port	*port*
bus	*bus*	ticket	*ticéad*

Best places to see

1 Christal Church Cathedral

www.cccdub.ie

Dublin's oldest stone building and stronghold of the Protestant faith in Ireland was saved from ruin by extensive Victorian restoration.

Built on the site of the Norse king Sitric Silkenbeard's wooden church of 1038, this Romanesque and early Gothic church was commissioned in 1172 by Richard de Clare, the Anglo-Norman conqueror of Dublin – better known as Strongbow – for Archbishop Laurence O'Toole. The archbishop later became St Laurence, patron of Dublin, whose heart remains in the cathedral in a 13th-century metal casket.

After Henry VIII broke with Rome, Robert Castle, the last prior of the Augustinian priory of Holy Trinity, became the first dean of Christ Church in 1541. In 1562 the nave roof vaulting collapsed, crushing Strongbow's tomb and leaving the cathedral in ruins. Temporary measures to shore up the damage remained in place until the 1870s, and the roof, to the present day, still leans out by 46cm (18in). During the 16th and 17th centuries Christ Church's crypt was used as a market, a meeting place and even a pub. Heavy restoration at the expense of Henry Roe, a local whiskey distiller, was

undertaken by architect George Edmund Street in the 1870s. Although little remains of the original Norman structure – only the south transept and the crypt – the cathedral was saved from complete decay. Further work took place in the 1980s and 1990s, including the restoration of the 12th-century crypt. This contains an intriguing range of relics and objects, including the old wooden punishment stocks. The exhibition 'Treasures of Christ Church' reflects 1,000 years of history, architecture and worship in Ireland.

✠ 20J ✉ Christchurch Place ☎ 677 8099 🕓 Jun–Aug daily 9–6; Sep–May daily 9:45–5. Treasures: Mon–Fri 9:45–5, Sat 10–4:45, Sun 12:30–3:15 ✋ Moderate 🚌 50, 51B, 78A, 123; Luas Four Courts

Dublin Castle and Chester Beatty Library

www.dublincastle.ie
www.cbl.ie

Situated on a strategic ridge, the castle is at the heart of historic Dublin. Visit the gallery and library in the gardens.

Dublin Castle was the headquarters of British rule for more than 700 years. Little remains of the original structure, except for the modified Record Tower containing the Garda (Police) Museum, and the mixture of architectural styles and government offices masks the fact that this was a Viking fortress. The castle stands on the site of the black pool or *dubh linn* from which the city took its name.

Following a fire in 1684, stately accommodation was built to replace the medieval interior, including the lavish Throne Room and the Ballroom or St Patrick's Hall, where the ceiling fresco is the most important painted ceiling in Ireland. The neo-Gothic Chapel Royal was added in 1807 and displays carved stone likenesses of a hundred British dignitaries. The Undercroft was revealed after excavations in 1990 and can be visited on a tour. Here you will see part of the original Viking fortress and, in the base of the Norman Powder Tower, some of the Viking defensive bank.

The **Chester Beatty Library** is housed in the Clock Tower Building and has a rich collection of artistic treasures from the great cultures and religions of the world. The manuscripts, prints, icons, books and other objects were bequeathed to the nation in 1956 by Sir Alfred Chester Beatty (1875–1968). This successful American mining magnate became one of the few people to have been made an honorary citizen of Ireland.

Dublin Castle

✚ 20J ✉ Castle Street ☎ Castle: 677 7129. Garda Museum: 666 9998 🕐 Mon–Fri 10–4:45, Sat–Sun 2–4:45. Closed during state business. Garda Museum: Mon–Fri 9:30–4:30 ✋ Moderate 🍴 Castle Vaults Bistro (€–€€) 🚌 Cross-city buses

Chester Beatty Library

✚ 21J ✉ Dublin Castle ☎ 407 0750 🕐 Mon–Fri 10–5, Sat 11–5, Sun 1–5. Closed Mon, Oct–Apr ✋ Free 🍴 Silk Road Café (€) 🚌 Cross-city buses

3 General Post Office

A significant building in the history of modern Ireland, the GPO was the main stronghold of the Irish Volunteers during the Easter Rising of 1916.

The imposing Palladian-style General Post Office in O'Connell Street was built in 1818, and while it is not one of Dublin's finest Georgian buildings, it is important in the history of Irish independence. It was from the steps of this building that Pádraic Pearse (1879–1916), leader of Irish nationalism, proclaimed Ireland a republic and no longer subject to British rule. He and his fellow volunteers resisted the British in a siege that lasted a week. Heavy bombardment forced the rebels out and the building was left severely damaged. The leaders of the uprising

were rounded up and 16 rebels were executed at Kilmainham Gaol (► 46–47), but the struggle against British rule continued and the siege at the Post Office highlights those years of struggle. The Irish Free State was finally formed five years later, in 1921.

The building, headquarters of An Post, the Irish Postal Service, re-opened in 1929. Despite heavy restoration, bullet holes can still be seen on the exterior walls. The building is a cross between a memorial to those who died and an everyday busy post office. Take a look inside at the remarkable bronze statue of the *Death of Cuchulainn* (by Oliver Sheppard, 1935), which depicts the demise of the legendary Irish hero Cuchulainn, and is dedicated to Pearse and the others who died in the Easter Rising. Note also the series of paintings depicting the Rising, in the manner of Communist propaganda posters. The building remains the focus of official parades and a salute is given here at Dublin's annual St Patrick's Day parade.

✚ 22H ✉ O'Connell Street ☎ 705 7000
🕐 Mon–Sat 8–8 🎟 Free 🚆 Tara Street
🚌 Cross-city buses; Luas Abbey Street

4 Guinness Storehouse

www.guinness-storehouse.com

Every visitor to Dublin should sample at least one pint of the 'black stuff'. The Storehouse is the ideal place to do this and learn about its production at the same time.

Guinness is synonymous with Dublin, an institution, a dominant employer in the city for more than two centuries and now a household name throughout the world. When Arthur Guinness decided to experiment with the English dark porter ale in 1759, little did he know that 200 years later his surname would be revered the world over. Indeed, the largest producer of Guinness is now Nigeria.

The Storehouse, opened in 2000 on the site of the original St James's Gate brewery, pays homage to the memory of that early discovery. The stunning glass central atrium, an innovative structure built into the historic building, is in the shape of a giant pint glass. The froth at the top of the pint is the Gravity Bar where you can sup your free pint at the end of your self-guided tour while enjoying panoramic views over the city. As you make your way up the pint glass you will go through the various production processes. The heady aroma of roasting hops pervades the air and you can touch and smell the individual ingredients. The water used in the production of Guinness is traditionally believed to come from the River Liffey; in fact it comes from the nearby Grand Canal. Further displays, all well labelled and some interactive, include machinery and transport vehicles. Check out the excellent advertising section, including examples of posters depicting the memorable toucan and the famous 1929 advert proclaiming 'Guinness is Good for You'.

🕂 17K 🖂 St James's Gate ☎ 408 4800 🕔 Daily 9:30–5 (9:30–7, Jul–Aug) 👋 Expensive 🍴 Gravity Bar, Source Bar, Brewery Bar and restaurant (€–€€) 🚌 51B, 78A, 123 🚊 Luas St James's ❓ Shop selling Guinness memorabilia

5 James Joyce Centre

www.jamesjoyce.ie

The centre is dedicated to fostering and promoting awareness of James Joyce's significant contribution to modern literature. Here you will find all manner of Joycean memorabilia.

James Joyce (1882–1941) spent most of his adult life in Europe, but it was his childhood in Dublin that provided him with the setting and characters for his novels *Ulysses*, *Finnegans Wake* and *Dubliners*. Joyce did not live in this particular house but in the vicinity, which was at the time a run-down area with most houses needing repair. In 1982 Senator David Norris restored the 18th-century town house to its original glory and converted it into a centre of Joycean study. Among the most interesting exhibits is a fascinating set of biographies of some 50 characters from the most famous of Joyce's works, *Ulysses*, written between 1914 and 1921.

The centre organizes walking tours so you can trace the footsteps of the novel's hero, Leopold Bloom, as he walked around the city on 16 June, 1904. During 2004, the centenary celebrations of

i have a special knack of putting the noose once in he can't get out

Terence o'ryan heard him and straightway brought him a crystal cup full of the foaming ebon ale

this event included special Bloomsday festivities throughout the city and around the world. Rejoyce 2004 also marked several months of activities and events based around the great master of the novel.

The James Joyce Centre also shows short films on Joyce and his Dublin, as well as recordings of him reading his own novels, and is now home to highlights from the National Library's 2004–06 landmark James Joyce and *Ulysses* exhibition. Look out for the murals around the courtyard depicting the 18 chapters of *Ulysses*, painted by Paul Joyce, great-nephew of James Joyce. You can also see the original door of No 7 Eccles Street, the fictional home of Leopold Bloom, and Joyce's death mask.

✚ 10E ✉ 35 North Great George's Street ☎ 878 8547
🕐 Tue–Sat 10–5 ✋ Moderate; tours expensive 🍴 Café
(€) 🚌 Cross-city buses ❓ Bookshop

6 Kilmainham Gaol

The gaol (jail) provides a moving insight into the grim reality of incarceration in Dublin's notorious prison. It remains a symbol of Ireland's fight for independence.

Inspired by the Bastille in Paris, Kilmainham Gaol was built in 1787, and remained a prison until 1924. It has held some of the most famous rebels in Ireland's history, including those from the rebellions of 1798, 1803, 1848, 1867, 1883 and, most famously, the 1916 Easter Rising. Visits are by guided tour only and start with a video presentation to set the grisly scene. The tour, which takes about 90 minutes, places the historical facts in context, emphasizing that this was a prison for civil as well as political prisoners. Petty criminals were also incarcerated here, including many victims of the Great Famine of 1845–49, when stealing was rife. Up to 7,000 inmates, both men and women, were crammed into the dank and dark cells.

The prison closed in 1910 and was converted into barracks to house troops during World War I, but it was re-opened to receive the insurgents of the 1916 Easter Rising. The public execution of 16 of the rebels that took place here included Joseph Plunkett, who married Grace Gifford just 10 minutes before his execution. The last prisoner to be held here, in 1924, was Eámon de Valera, who went on to become president of Ireland. The abandoned gaol fell into decay, but because of its exceptional historical interest was restored by volunteer groups in the 1960s.

Among the areas included on the tour are the east- and west-wing cell blocks, the chapel, the exercise yard where the rebels were executed and the museum with its grim artefacts and Irish memorabilia.

✠ 13K ✉ Inchicore Road, Kilmainham ☎ 453 5984
🕐 Apr–Sep daily 9:30–5; Oct–Mar Mon–Sat 9:30–5, Sun and public hols 10–6. Last tour 1 hour before closing
✋ Moderate 🍽 Tea room (€) 🚌 51B, 78A; Luas Suir Road
❓ Guided tours only – reservations advisable

7

National Gallery

www.nationalgallery.ie

Home to one of Europe's premier collections of Old Masters, the National Gallery also displays home-grown talent, in particular the works of the Yeats family.

The gallery opened its doors to the public in 1864, in a building designed by Francis Fowke, the architect of the Victoria & Albert Museum in London. Beginning with just 125 paintings, the gallery's prime task was to inspire Irish artists of the day. The collection now has more than 2,500 paintings and some 10,000 works in different media, including drawings, prints and sculptures.

The building consists of four wings: the original Dargan Wing, the Milltown Wing, the Beit Wing, and the Millennium Wing housing a study centre of Irish work and temporary exhibition galleries.

The collections are vast and can be confusing, so pick up a floor plan. You may want to single out your own personal favourites rather than wander round each gallery. In the Millennium Wing is a multimedia gallery with computer touch screens where you can find out background information on paintings in the collection. Every major European school of painting is represented here. If it's Old Masters you're after, look for works by Fra Angelico, Titian, Caravaggio, Rembrandt and Canova. Lovers of Impressionism can view works by Monet, Degas, Pissarro, Sisley and others. British artists such as Reynolds and Turner are also represented, as are modern painters up to Picasso. A recent acquisition is Van Gogh's *Rooftops of Paris*.

Among the works of Jack B Yeats in the Yeats Museum are several Dublin cityscapes.

✚ 23K ✉ Merrion Square West and Clare Street ☎ 661 5133 🕔 Mon–Sat 9:30–5:30, Thu 9:30–8:30, Sun 12–5:30 ✋ Free; expensive for special exhibitions 🍴 Restaurant and café (€–€€) 🚇 Pearse 🚌 Cross-city buses ❓ Guided tours Sat 3pm, Sun 2, 3 and 4pm; audio tour

8 National Museum

www.museum.ie

Ireland's rich heritage is brought to life in this superb building, one of Dublin's foremost attractions, with some of the best gold artefacts on display in Europe.

The collections are exhibited in a magnificent building of 1877. The splendid domed rotunda, which forms the entrance hall, has columns of Irish marble and a mosaic floor depicting the signs of the zodiac. This is the national repository for more than 2 million artefacts dating from 7000BC to the late medieval period.

Beginning with the prehistoric period, you will

find displays of tools and weaponry from the Stone and Bronze ages. Check out the 13m (42ft) Lurgan longboat. Dating from around 2500BC, it is Ireland's earliest surviving boat, hewn out of an oak tree. Other artefacts are in excellent condition, having been preserved in Ireland's peat bogs. The stunning Bronze Age gold jewellery of the 'Ór – Ireland's Gold' exhibition is unmatched in Europe

and the styles, surprisingly sophisticated, are still copied today. In the Treasury you can see several 8th-century gems including the Ardagh Chalice, a beautiful, gilded, twin-handled cup, and the stunning Tara brooch, intricately decorated with birds and animals. Look out for the gilt-bronze 12th-century Cross of Cong, with its silver wire, crystals and enamelled studs. On the same floor, the Road to Independence exhibition is a vivid portrayal of Ireland's turbulent political history from 1900 to the signing of the Anglo-Irish treaty of 1921.

Upstairs are the Viking Age Ireland and Medieval Ireland 1150–1550 collections, perhaps a little more down to earth after the magnificence of the earlier displays. The Clothes from Bogs in Ireland exhibition gathers together all the historic clothing found incredibly well preserved in Irish wetlands and bogs.

✚ 23K ✉ Kildare Street ☎ 677 7444 🕐 Tue–Sat 10–5, Sun 2–5 💷 Free 🍴 Café (€) 🚇 Pearse 🚌 Cross-city buses ❓ Guided tours from main entrance at regular intervals

9 St Patrick's Cathedral

www.stpatrickscathedral.ie

St Patrick's is Dublin's second great cathedral and the largest church in Ireland. It is a paradox that in a predominately Catholic city and country there should be two Protestant cathedrals.

Legend has it that St Patrick passed through Dublin on his travels in Ireland in the 5th century. A small wooden church was built on the spot where he converted several pagans to Christianity. On this same site the Anglo-Norman first bishop of Dublin, John Comyn, constructed a stone church, which was upgraded to cathedral status in 1219. It was built in the English Gothic style and finally completed in 1284. By the 19th century it was in a very poor state and lay almost derelict among slum housing. Much of the cathedral was rebuilt and restored between 1860 and 1900, paid for mainly by the Guinness family.

Just inside the building is the grave of one of the cathedral's most famous sons. The author and reformist Jonathan Swift

Limerick County Library

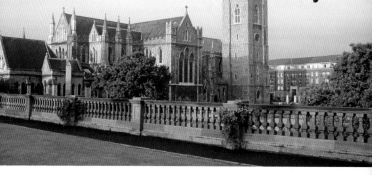

was dean here from 1713 to 1745 and he tried hard to preserve the building, but to no avail. The death mask, pulpit, chair and writing table of the great man are among memorabilia on display. Other highlights include the largest organ in the country, and you can also hear the largest peal of bells in Ireland. A particularly interesting memorial is the

one to the celebrated blind harpist Turlough O'Carolan (1670–1730). The exhibition 'Living Stones' celebrates the cathedral's role in city life and its place in the history of Dublin. It is important to remember that St Patrick's is not a museum but very much an active church and an integral part of city life.

✚ 20K ✉ Patrick's Street ☎ 453 9472 ◷ Mar–Oct Mon–Sat 9–5, Sun 9–11, 12:45–3, 4:15–6; Nov–Feb Mon–Sat 9–5, Sun 10–11, 12:45–3 ✋ Moderate
🚌 Cross-city buses

10 Trinity College and the Book of Kells

www.tcd.ie

The oldest university in Ireland houses the Book of Kells, arguably one of the most

beautifully illuminated manuscripts in the world.

Trinity College is a peaceful oasis amid the hustle and bustle of modern Dublin. The main entrance on College Green is next to one of the busiest roads in Dublin, but once inside you enter a different world. Parliament Square, with its 19th-century campanile and elegant 18th-century Dining Hall and Chapel, leads on to Fellows' Square, where old and new buildings blend sympathetically. The Old Library (1732), designed by Thomas Burgh, stands to the west; to the east is Benjamin Woodward's 19th-century carved Museum building; to the south Paul Koralek's New Library (1978).

Most visitors head straight for the Old Library to see the magnificent Book of Kells and other ancient illuminated manuscripts, housed in the darkened Treasury on the ground floor. Written on vellum around AD800, the Book of Kells is a superbly illustrated transcription of the Gospels. The exhibition 'Turning Darkness into Light' explains the

context of the book and how the monastic scribes produced such a sublime work of art, highly imaginative, with figures of humans and animals, and intricate Celtic patterns. It was discovered in the town of Kells in County Meath, but is thought to have been created by four Irish monks on Iona, off the coast of Scotland. Apparently they fled from the Vikings to Ireland and finished the book in Kells. Two volumes can usually be seen, one opened to display the decorative work and one showing script. Other ornate manuscripts are on show.

The Long Room, upstairs from the Treasury, is nearly 65m (213ft) in length and houses around 200,000 books. The 15th-century harp on display here, believed to be the oldest in Ireland, is the harp that appears on Irish coins.

🕇 22J 🖂 College Street ☎ College: 896 1000; library: 896 1661 🕔 College campus daily. Old Library and Book of Kells: May–Sep Mon–Sat 9:30–5, Sun 9:30–4:30; Oct–Apr 12–4:30 🖐 Campus free; Old Library and Book of Kells expensive 🚇 Tara Street 🚌 Cross-city buses ❓ College tours May–Sep. Douglas Hyde Gallery for temporary art exhibitions all year

Best things to do

Great places to have lunch

Avoca (€)

A popular spot for wholesome home-made food or a light salad. Scrumptious desserts and good coffee. On the top floor of the Avoca department store.

✉ 11–13 Suffolk Street ☎ 677 4215; www.avoca.ie

Bad Ass Café (€)

Drop in for a burger or pizza at this well-known, unpretentious café in Temple Bar that has been appealing to young Dubliners for more than 20 years.

✉ 9–11 Crown Alley ☎ 671 2596; www.badasscafe.com

Bewley's Oriental Café (€–€€)

You can't visit Dublin without taking a break in the legendary surroundings of Bewley's (▶ 105).

✉ 78 Grafton Street ☎ 672 7720; www.bewleys.com

Brazen Head (€€)

Traditional old-world pub where the lunch-time carvery is a tempting option (► 97).

✉ 20 Bridge Street Lower ☎ 679 5186; www.brazenhead.com

Café Mao (€€)

Try the delicious stir-fries at this lively restaurant serving the best in Asian food.

✉ 2–3 Chatham Row ☎ 670 4899; www.cafemao.com

Eden (€€)

Pristine restaurant overlooking busy Meeting House Square in Temple Bar, serving excellent modern Irish cuisine.

✉ Meeting House Square ☎ 670 5372; www.edenrestaurant.ie

Guinea Pig Fish Restaurant (€€€)

If you want to get out of town and sample the freshest fish, try this family-run seaside establishment.

✉ 17 Railway Road, Dalkey ☎ 285 9055; www.guineapig.dalkey.info

Leo Burdock's (€)

If you haven't the time or inclination to eat in, this classic take-away fish-and-chip shop has been frying since 1913.

✉ 2 Werburgh Street ☎ 454 0306

Nude (€)

Help do your bit for the environment at this eco-friendly eatery, which serves healthy options.

✉ 21 Suffolk Street ☎ 677 5577

Queen of Tarts (€)

Enjoy excellent home cooking here, including mouth-watering sweet and savoury pastries and great sandwiches.

✉ 4 Cork Hill, Dame Street ☎ 670 7499

Great pubs

The Brazen Head is said to be the oldest pub in Dublin, serving for some 800 years.
✉ 20 Bridge Street Lower ☎ 679 5186

Davy Byrnes has strong literary connections with James Joyce.
✉ 21 Duke Street ☎ 677 5217

Doheny & Nesbitt is a glorious old pub frequented by politicians and journalists.
✉ 5 Lower Baggot Street ☎ 676 2945

The Long Hall, where time has stood still, is ornately Victorian and has an exceptionally long bar.
✉ 51 South Great George's Street ☎ 475 1590

McDaid's, once a morgue and a Moravian chapel, was popular with literary giants – Brendan Behan and friends drank here.
✉ 3 Harry Street ☎ 679 4395

Mulligan's, established in 1782, serves one of the best pints of Guinness in the city.
✉ 8 Poolbeg Street ☎ 677 5582

O'Donoghue's has been entertaining generations of Dubliners with its traditional music and great *craic*.
✉ 15 Merrion Row ☎ 660 7194

Oliver St John Gogarty is popular with tourists but it still retains its traditional ambience with Irish music and good local food.
✉ 58–59 Fleet Street ☎ 671 1822

The Porterhouse is one of the few bars in Ireland to brew its own beer. It also has a large selection of imported beers.
✉ 16–18 Parliament Street ☎ 679 8847

The Stag's Head in the heart of Georgian Dublin has wonderful period features.
✉ 1 Dame Court ☎ 679 3701

Statues and sculptures

A bronze of James Joyce in casual pose, complete with obligatory hat and walking stick, can be found at the western end of Earl Street.

The Children of Lír in the Garden of Remembrance. Oisín Kelly's evocative bronze is dedicated to those who died in the pursuit of Irish independence.

Daniel O'Connell, the 'Liberator', dominates the end of O'Connell Street, near the O'Connell Bridge, where this imposing monument was erected in 1882.

Famine Figures on the Custom House Quay commemorate the suffering of the Irish people during the Great Famine of 1845–49.

The Fusiliers' Arch at the entrance to St Stephen's Green is a tribute to the Royal Dublin Fusiliers who were lost in the Boer War.

Meeting Place by Jakki Mckenna, next to the northern end of the Ha'penny Bridge, is known locally as the 'Hags with the Bags'.

Molly Malone hasn't escaped the wit of the nickname-giving Dubliners – the bronze 'Tart with the Cart' still plies her cockles and mussels in Lower Grafton Street.

A colourful statue of Oscar Wilde reclines languorously on a rock in Merrion Square, close to the house where he lived from 1855 to 1876.

Patrick Kavanagh, the poet, sits in meditation on a bench by the leafy Grand Canal.

The Viking Boat on Essex Quay by Betty Maguire reflects on the city's Viking origins.

Guided tours

Dublin Castle
The guided tour of Dublin Castle leads through sumptuous state apartments that are the scene of Irish ceremonial occasions such as presidential inaugurations and receptions for visiting heads of state. It ends in the Viking depths of the undercroft, where you see part of the original city wall.

Ghostbus
A scary two-and-a-quarter-hour trip on board a spooky bus, with actors leading the way to a twilight world of ghosts, ghouls and gruesome happenings.
☎ 703 3028 for reservations; www.dublinbus.ie

Historical Walking Tours of Dublin
Explore the rich history of this ancient city in the company of Trinity College history students. You will learn about political history and tour locations that featured in key events in Ireland's history. Several themed walks are available.
☎ 87 688 9412 for information; www.historicalinsights.ie

Literary Pub Crawl
This two-hour tour is led by a couple of actors, who bring to life the words of the featured writers while guiding you to four of the pubs made famous by the likes of James Joyce, Samuel Beckett, W B Yeats, Brendan Behan and Oscar Wilde. Combines fun, books, history and good beer.
☎ 670 5602 for information; www.dublinpubcrawl.com

Musical Pub Crawl
Traditional Irish music is popular the world over, and the musicians who lead this tour are both professional and knowledgeable. You will visit renowned music pubs, learn about the music tradition and finish up at a lively session. Starts from Oliver St John Gogarty.
☎ 475 3313 for information; www.discoverdublin.ie

1916 Rebellion Walking Tours

Learn more about this critical part of Ireland's history by joining this first-class walking tour that runs from March to October. The two-hour daily tours start from the International Bar at 23 Wicklow Street and are taken by the authors of the book, *The Easter Rising*.
☎ 86 858 3847; www.1916rising.com

Rock 'n' Roll Stroll

Some legendary modern musicians have called Dublin home, and this self-guided tour takes in a number of places connected with them. You'll see where Phil Lynott played before Thin Lizzy whisked him to stardom, where Sinéad O'Connor was a waitress and the recording studios where rock icons U2 have cut albums. Pick up the leaflet from any tourist office in the city.

St Michan's Crypt

This ordinary church north of the river has a secret, and if you join one of the low-key guided tours you can discover what lurks under the surface. The crypt of the church contains mummified remains of a number of bodies, some of which date back many centuries. You can actually see some of the oldest of them, and the tour guide gives an entertaining account of these and other remains.

Best views

The Chimney at Smithfield (➤ 151)

The Gravity Bar, Guinness Storehouse (➤ 42–43)

Howth Head, Howth (➤ 171)

James Joyce Tower, Sandycove (➤ 177)

St Michael's Tower, Dvblinia (➤ 84)

Beautiful bridges

Father Matthew Bridge

Ha'penny Bridge

James Joyce Bridge

Millennium Bridge

O'Connell Bridge

Sean O'Casey Bridge

Places to be entertained

Abbey Theatre

Internationally renowned theatre, staging the works of classic Irish writers such as Sean O'Casey, George Bernard Shaw, Brendan Behan and W B Yeats. The downstairs Peacock Theatre stages experimental works, many by up-and-coming Irish writers.

✉ 26 Abbey Street ☎ 878 7222

Comedy Night at The International

Local and international stand-up acts pack out the tiny upstairs room at The International bar Thursday to Saturday.

✉ Wicklow Street ☎ 677 9250

Gaiety Theatre

The focus here is on mainstream drama by Irish playwrights, plus musicals, ballet, opera and pantomime. Old black and white movies are screened here sometimes, and after the plays are over the building becomes a nightclub offering themed music nights (salsa, R&B, soul, etc).

✉ 5 King Street South ☎ 677 1717

Gate Theatre

Critically acclaimed theatre offering modern Irish and international plays (➤ 142).

✉ 1 Cavendish Row ☎ 874 4045

Irish Film Centre

The place to go for art-house, independent and foreign films.

✉ 6 Eustace Street, Temple Bar ☎ 679 5744

National Concert Hall

This is the home of the National Symphony Orchestra, on stage every Friday from November to May, plus visiting opera, chamber music, jazz and dance ensembles.

✉ Earlsfort Terrace ☎ 417 0077

Olympia Theatre

This is a nice old theatre that serves up a programme of popular comedies and drama, with a pantomime at Christmas. Occasional concerts by Irish bands.

✉ 72 Dame Street
☎ 677 7744

The Point

This huge concert hall in the redeveloped docklands is now the city's foremost concert venue, hosting blockbuster events, including solo stars and international bands. Undergoing renovation.

✉ East Link Toll Bridge, North Wall ☎ 836 3633

Spirit Nightclub

This is more than a DJ dance club – it hosts such big-name performers as David Bowie, Van Morrison, Westlife, Nina Simone and Suzanne Vega.

✉ 57 Abbey Street Middle ☎ 884 3633

Temple Bar

This is the hub of Dublin's nightlife scene, with the greatest concentration of nightclubs and music. The best plan is just to wander around and see what sounds take your fancy.

Best buys

Art and antiques
Scour the city's contemporary art galleries for works by local artists, or perhaps pick up a piece of Irish silver (look for the harp hallmark) at one of the many antiques shops.

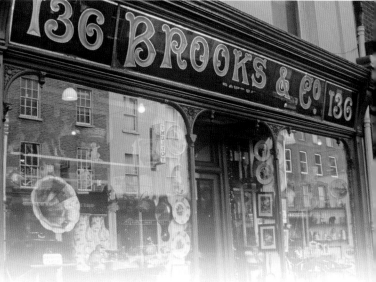

Books
Bookshops, such as the one at the Dublin Writers Museum or the Winding Stair Bookshop, sell a superlative range of books, including works by Irish writers and on Irish themes.

Celtic crafts
There's an enormous range of works by Irish craftspeople, including delicate jewellery based on ancient Celtic designs, fine pottery and sturdy, hand-thrown ceramics, wood carvings and items made from Connemara marble. Tourist information centres,

department stores and quality craft shops have authentic items, as opposed to the tourist stuff found in some outlets.

Drink
A bottle of Irish whiskey makes a great souvenir; Bushmills and Jamesons are well-known brands, so seek out one that's not so widely available internationally, such as Paddy or Powers.

Fashion
A number of Irish fashion designers are gaining international acclaim, including Louise Kennedy (formal suits), Orla Kiely (bags), Philip Treacy (hats) and Vivienne Walsh (jewellery). Look for their work in the Design Centre, Brown Thomas or the Kilkenny shop.

Food
Irish smoked salmon travels well, and there are some wonderful farmhouse cheeses, such as Durrus, Cashel Blue and Gubbeen.

Glass
Waterford Crystal is world-famous, and is available, along with pieces from other Irish glass makers, in all the major gift shops and department stores.

Irish woollens
High-quality woven and knitted garments are not confined to the chunky Aran sweaters; there are also sophisticated fashion knits created by trendy Dublin designers, such as Lainey Keogh.

Music
There's nothing like a shot of atmospheric traditional music to bring back memories of your visit, and there are a number of music shops that have recordings. Claddagh Records, in Temple Bar's Cecilia Street, is particularly good, or try Celtic Note on Kildare Street.

a walk along the Liffey Quays

Start from the magnificent Custom House (➤ 138–139) and follow along the quay west to O'Connell Bridge. After the bridge, stroll along the boardwalk by the side of the Liffey until you reach the Ha'penny Bridge (➤ 84–85), one of the oldest cast-iron structures of its kind in the world. Don't miss the sculpture of two shoppers chatting on a bench; known as the 'Hags with the Bags', its official name is Meeting Place. Cross the bridge and turn right into Wellington Quay.

This quay was the last to be built, in 1812, and is lined with tall narrow merchants' houses. Its most notable building is the Clarence Hotel (➤ 96), converted from the 19th-century former Custom House and now very popular with celebrities.

Continue along the quay and glance left down Parliament Street where you can see the striking City Hall (➤ 82–83) built in 1769. On the other side of Parliament Street you pass the Sunlight Chambers (➤ 89). Look for the attractive terracotta frieze on the building. You are now in Essex Quay.

Check out Betty Maguire's bronze *Viking Boat* sculpture. This was the area first settled by the Vikings in the 9th century.

Go past the Dublin Council offices on your left and head along Merchant's Quay. Glance across the water to the stunning Four Courts building (➤ 141), considered

by many to be the finest public building in Dublin.
Turn left into Bridge Street Lower. On your right is
the Brazen Head.

This pub, the oldest in Dublin, has been serving for more
than 800 years, although the current building dates only
from the 17th century.

Distance 1.5km (1 mile)
Time 1 hour
Start point Custom House, Custom House Quay ✚ 23H
End point Brazen Head, 20 Bridge Street Lower ✚ 19J
Lunch Brazen Head (➤ 59)

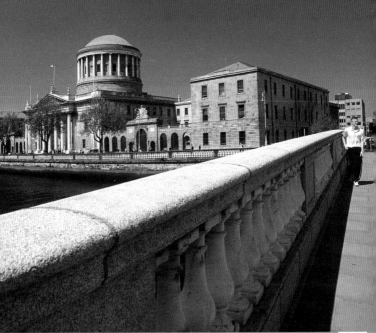

Sporting events

Six Nations Rugby Tournament (February)
The Irish leg of this hard-fought tournament – between Ireland, England, Wales, Scotland, France and Italy – takes place at Croke Park while the Lansdowne Road Stadium is being redeveloped.
✉ St Joseph's Avenue ☎ 819 2300 🚌 11, 16, 51A

Colours Boat Race (April)
Rowers from Trinity College and University College compete over a River Liffey course.

All Ireland Hurling Final (September)
The ancient sport of hurling is uniquely Celtic and is enthusiastically supported.

All-Ireland Gaelic Football Final (September)
Gaelic football looks like a cross between soccer and rugby, but is said to pre-date both of those games. The All-Ireland championship is a very important fixture in Ireland's sporting calendar.

Dublin City Marathon (October)
This long-established marathon is extremely popular, and is renowned as one of the most friendly city marathons in the world.

Leopardstown Christmas National Hunt Festival (December)
The Irish have a particular love of horse racing, and around 65,000 of them attend this four-day Christmas Festival, south of the city.

Activities

Cycling Dublin is perfect for cycling; it's relatively compact and mostly flat. If you want to escape the crowded streets, Phoenix Park is ideal, or if you're feeling more ambitious you could cycle out to the coast at Howth or Dalkey. Irish Cycling Safaris (tel: 260 0749; www.cyclingsafaris.com), at the Belfield Bike Shop, University College Dublin, organizes cycling tours.

Fishing Dublin is well placed for great beach and pier fishing at various points around the bay, and fishing charter boats head out to sea from Dun Laoghaire. There's fishing on the Grand and Royal canals (call the Dublin Angling Initiative on 087 674 0214).

Golf There are more than 60 courses within easy reach of Dublin. The most famous are Ireland's oldest golf club, Royal Dublin (tel: 833 6346), and Portmarnock (tel: 846 2968), created by Bernhard Langer. A complete list of private courses can be obtained from the Golfing Union of Ireland (tel: 505 4000; www.gui.ie)

Hiking The 132km (82-mile) Wicklow Way stretches from Dublin over the Wicklow Mountains to Clonegal in Co Carlow. The walk starts in Marlay Park, just outside Dublin, and continues along forest tracks and country roads to valleys and lakes, and ultimately to the highest village in Ireland, Roundwood.

Horse-back riding The Wicklow Mountains offer some wonderful trekking opportunities. The Devil's Glen Equestrian Village in Ashford, Co Wicklow, organizes treks through the rolling hills or down to the beach (tel: 0404 40637; www.devilsglen.ie).

Places to take the children

The Ark
This cultural centre aimed at children of all ages offers stimulating performances for children in the indoor theatre, outdoor amphitheatre (summer only) and workshop space.

✉ 11a Eustace Street, Temple Bar ☎ 670 7788; www.ark.ie 🕓 Mon–Fri 10–5; call for activity times 🚉 Tara Street 🚌 Cross-city buses

Bram Stoker Dracula Experience
See page 135.

The Chimney
See page 151.

Clara Lara Fun Park
An adventure park set in woodland and lakes in the Wicklow Mountains. Fun rides, mostly involving water, include Aqua Shuttle, rafts and boats. Or there are go-karts, woodland play areas and assault courses.

✉ Vale of Clara, Rathdrum, Co Wicklow ☎ 0404 46161; www.claralara.com 🕓 May–Sep daily 10:30–6 💰 Expensive

Dublin Zoo
See pages 140–141.

Dvblinia and the Viking World
See page 84.

Fry Model Railway
A 240sq m (2,580sq ft) railway layout that displays the unique collection of hand-made models of Irish trains, from the beginning of rail travel to the present day.

✉ Malahide Castle, Malahide ☎ 846 3779 🕓 Apr–Sep Mon–Thu, Sat 10–1, 2–5, Sun and public hols 2–6 💰 Moderate 🚉 Malahide (then 10-min walk) 🚌 42

Lambert Puppet Theatre

This puppet theatre delights children with imaginative and enjoyable re-enactments of famous fairy-tales.

✉ 5 Clifton Lane, Monkstown ☎ 280 0974; www.lambertpuppettheatre.com ⏰ Performances Sat, Sun 3:30; or by arrangement for groups 💰 Expensive 🚇 Monkstown/Salthill 🚌 7, 7A

National Sea Life Centre

The main attraction is the 'Lair of the Octopus', a re-creation of the undersea world inhabited by these strange beasts. Or have a close encounter with sea horses, sharks or giant Japanese spider crabs.

✉ Strand Road, Bray ☎ 286 6939; www.sealifeeurope.com ⏰ Daily from 10am; call for display times and winter openings 💰 Expensive 🚇 Bray (5-min walk) 🚌 45, 84

Newgrange Farm

Kids will love this hands-on farm where they can feed the animals and view the exotic birds in the aviary. The farmer demonstrates

how to shoe a horse and you can see sheepdogs at work. Every Sunday the 'sheep derby' takes place: a highly amusing race where teddies are used as jockeys and each child is allocated a sheep to support. Best visited by car as public transport serving the farm is limited.

✉ Newgrange, between Drogheda and Slane ☎ 041 982 4119 ⏰ Easter–Aug daily 10–6 💰 Moderate

Viking Splash Tours

Fun and educational, this tour takes you through Viking Dublin aboard a reconditioned World War II amphibious bus before ploughing into the Grand Canal to conclude the trip on water. Departs from Bull Alley and St Stephen's Green North.

✉ 64–65 Patrick Street ☎ 707 6000; www.vikingsplash.ie ⏰ Feb to mid-Nov regular daily tours (call for times) 💰 Expensive

Exploring

Dublin is a small city and very easy to explore. Walking is the best option, although there is an excellent bus service. The River Liffey provides a prominent landmark when navigating the city and most attractions are on the south side, including Temple Bar, Grafton Street, Trinity College and the Georgian district, with its renowned national museums and galleries. North of the river has always been considered the poor relation, but with restoration projects being carried out at Smithfield Village, O'Connell Street/Henry Street and the docks, it's taking on a smarter image. The renovation of Dublin is ongoing, with parts of the city seemingly forever under scaffolding. After dark, serious partygoers head for Temple Bar and its pubs and bars; it also has a wide selection of restaurants. For those who prefer a quieter evening, there are plenty of sophisticated restaurants, trendy bars and low-key pubs.

Southside West

**This part of
Dublin is one
of the most
historic and
fascinating
areas in the city,
the place where the
earliest Celtic settlers set
up home, where the Vikings
created their city more than 1,000 years ago and
where, according to legend, St Patrick embarked on his
mission to convert the Irish to Christianity. Here you
will find some of the finest historic buildings, including
the two medieval cathedrals (Christ Church and St
Patrick's), Dublin Castle, the ceremonial heart of the
modern Republic of Ireland, and the sombre and
sobering Kilmainham Gaol.**

War Memorial
Gardens

KILMAINHAM

Here too is one of the most vibrant areas of the city, the warren
of narrow cobbled streets known as
Temple Bar. Once a derelict, down-at-
heel docklands area it's now home
to trendy shops and galleries, pubs
and restaurants, music venues and
nightclubs – buzzing with activity at
any time of the day or night. Beyond
Temple Bar, most of the southwest
part of the city is neither picturesque
nor happening, but it draws visitors
by the thousand because it contains
one of the most famous institutions
in Dublin – the Guinness Brewery
and its interpretative centre, the
Guinness Storehouse.

CHRIST CHURCH CATHEDRAL

Best places to see, ➤ 36–37.

CITY HALL

This imposing building, with its striking Corinthian portico, was originally designed by Thomas Cooley between 1769 and 1779 to house the Royal Exchange, and became the headquarters of the Dublin Corporation in 1852. In 2000 the interior of the building was restored to its former Georgian magnificence. It's worth going inside just to admire its superb rotunda, stunningly lit by the huge windows. In the vaulted basement the multimedia

exhibition 'The Story of the Capital' tells the story of Dublin from its beginnings to the present day, with special attention to the development of civic government. There are displays of civic regalia, including the Great City Sword and the Great Mace. You can trace the history of Dublin through invasion, rebellion, civil war and plague, and learn about the impact of the Viking, Norman, French-Huguenot and British rule on the city.

www.dublincity.ie/your_council/city_hall

✚ 21J ✉ Cork Hill, Dame Street
☎ 222 2204 🕐 Mon–Sat 10–5:15, Sun and public hols 2–5 ✋ Moderate
🚌 Cross-city buses

DRIMNAGH CASTLE

You need to search for this place because it's hidden behind school buildings on the western outskirts of Dublin. But it is worth the effort as Drimnagh Castle is an outstanding example of an old feudal stronghold. Until 1954 it was one of the oldest continually inhabited castles in Ireland. The only Irish castle to have a full moat, it is set in a wonderfully restored 17th-century garden. From the 1950s the castle was in a bad state of repair and was not restored until the 1980s, when traditional craft skills were used to return it to its former glory.

✚ 13L (off map) ✉ Long Mile Road, Drimnagh ☎ 450 2530 🕐 Wed 12–5, or by appointment ✋ Moderate 🚌 18, 77; Luas Drimnagh

DUBLIN CASTLE AND CHESTER BEATTY LIBRARY

Best places to see, ➤ 38–39.

DVBLINIA AND THE VIKING WORLD

This award-winning exhibition reproduces the sights and sounds of medieval Dublin. Housed in the former Synod Hall, it is joined to Christ Church Cathedral by a bridge. Note that the bridge is only one way – into the cathedral – so visit Dvblinia first. Experience medieval life through reconstructions of streets and houses. Major events in Dublin's history are re-created, including the Black Death and early rebellion. There are also artefacts removed from the excavation of nearby Wood Quay, which revealed Norse and Viking items. From the top of St Michael's Tower there are great views of the city. www.dublinia.ie

🕂 20J 🖂 St Michael's Hill, Christchurch ☎ 679 4611 🕓 Apr–Sep daily 10–5; Oct–Mar Mon–Sat 11–4:30, Sun and public hols 10–4:30 ✋ Expensive (including Christ Church) 🍴 Tea room Jun–Aug (€) 🚌 50, 51B, 78A; Luas Four Courts ❓ Pre-reservable tours available

GUINNESS STOREHOUSE

Best places to see, ➤ 42–43.

HA'PENNY BRIDGE

This central Dublin landmark, originally called the Wellington Bridge after the Duke of Wellington, opened in 1816. It gained its nickname because up until 1919 it cost a half penny to walk across the bridge. Before the opening of the new Millennium

Bridge in 2000 it was the only pedestrian bridge across the Liffey. The ornate, arched footbridge was renovated in 2001 and repainted its historically correct off-white. Three lamps supported by carved ironwork span the walkway which, together with the old-fashioned lampposts at either end, make the bridge particularly attractive when illuminated at night.

➕ 21H ✉ Between Liffey Street Lower (north side) and Crown Alley (south side) 🚆 Tara Street 🚌 Cross-city buses

IRISH JEWISH MUSEUM

The earliest reference to Jewish people in Ireland records the arrival of five Jews from 'over the sea' in 1079, but the first to settle here came from Portugal and Spain at the end of the 15th century, fleeing persecution and the Inquisition. The former synagogue in which this museum is housed retains many of its original features. The museum traces the history and the cultural, professional and commercial life of Dublin's small but active Jewish community. It also chronicles Jewish lives through paintings, books and photographs, and has a re-created kitchen scene showing a typical Sabbath meal from the early 1900s.

➕ 20M (off map) ✉ 4 Walworth Road ☎ 490 1857 🕐 May–Sep Tue, Thu, Sun 11–3:30; Oct–Apr Sun 10:30–2:30 🎫 Free 🚌 16, 16A, 19, 19A, 122

IRISH MUSEUM OF MODERN ART

The magnificent Royal Hospital building that houses the Irish Museum of Modern Art was designed by Sir William Robinson in 1684 for the Duke of Ormonde as a home for retired soldiers and was based on Les Invalides in Paris. It remained a home until 1927, and was finally restored in the 1980s. In 1991 it opened as the Irish Museum of Modern Art. Its stark grey-and-white interior provides a striking backdrop for the permanent collection of Irish and international modern and contemporary art. There are regular temporary exhibitions and a community programme covering music and the visual arts.

www.imma.ie

🟦 15J 🖂 Royal Hospital, Military Road, Kilmainham ☎ 612 9900
🕐 Tue–Sat 10–5:30, Sun and public hols 12–5:30 🖐 Free; guided tours Tue–Fri 10, 11:45, 2:30, 4: moderate 🍴 Café (€) 🚌 51B, 78A, 79, 90; Luas Heuston ❓ Formal gardens; bookshop

KILMAINHAM GAOL

Best places to see, ➤ 46–47.

MARSH'S LIBRARY

Ireland's oldest public library has remained virtually unchanged throughout its 300-year history. There are some 25,000 volumes dating from the 15th to early 18th century, plus manuscripts and maps. At the far end of the reading gallery are three alcoves, or 'cages', where scholars were locked in to stop them from stealing valuable tomes. The oldest book is Cicero's *Letters to his Friends*, published in 1472, and other highlights are signed copies of books by Jonathan Swift and English poet John Donne. Signatures in the guest book include those of James Joyce and Daniel O'Connell.

www.marshlibrary.ie

🟦 20K 🖂 St Patrick's Close ☎ 454 3511 🕐 Mon, Wed, Thu, Fri 10–1, 2–5, Sat 10:30–1 🖐 Inexpensive 🚌 Cross-city buses

ST AUDOEN'S CHURCHES

The two churches dedicated to St Audoen – originally known as St Ouen – bishop of Rouen and patron saint of Normandy, stand side by side in the heart of the old medieval city. The most interesting is the Protestant St Audoen's, the only surviving medieval parish church in Dublin. It is believed there has been a church here since the 9th century, but the tower and door of this version dates from the 12th century. The nave was added in the 15th century and three of the bells date from 1423. Look for the restored memorials to the Sparke and Duff families. An exhibition explaining the importance of St Audoen's in the life of medieval Dublin is on display in the Guild Chapel of St Anne. The adjoining Roman Catholic Church of St Audoen was built between 1841 and 1847.

🚏 19J ✉ Cornmarket, High Street ☎ 677 0088 🕐 Jun–Oct daily 9:30–5:30; call for winter times 💷 Inexpensive 🚌 Cross-city buses

ST PATRICK'S CATHEDRAL

Best places to see, ➤ 52–53.

SHAW'S BIRTHPLACE

'Author of many plays' is the simple accolade on the plaque outside the birthplace of George Bernard Shaw, the famous playwright. This restored Victorian home, close to the Grand Canal, reflects the life of a 19th-century middle-class family and was a source of inspiration for many of the characters Shaw would use later in his plays. You can see the drawing room where Shaw's mother held her musical soirees, the front parlour and the children's bedrooms. Shaw was born here in 1856, leaving 20 years later to live in London.

🞡 21M ✉ 33 Synge Street ☎ 475 0854
🕒 May–Sep Mon–Tue, Thu–Fri 10–1, 2–5,
Sat–Sun and public hols 2–5 💷 Expensive
🚌 16, 16A, 19, 19A

SUNLIGHT CHAMBERS

On the corner of Essex Quay and Parliament Street, on the south side of the river, stands Sunlight Chambers. It was built at the turn of the 20th century to be used as the Dublin offices of soap manufacturers Lever Brothers. Designed by Liverpool architect Edward Ould, who also designed Port Sunlight in England, the building has unusual Italianate terracotta friezes that advertise the company's product. In fact, they depict the history of hygiene. In its early years the building was unpopular because a 'foreign' architect had been employed, and upon its completion a journal called *The Irish Builder* referred to it as the 'ugliest building in Dublin'.

🞡 20J ✉ Essex Quay 🕒 View from outside only 🚌 Cross-city buses

TEMPLE BAR

The area known as Temple Bar is sandwiched between Dame Street and the River Liffey and covers some 11ha (27 acres). Its origins can be traced back to Anglo-Irish Sir William Temple, who bought the land bounding the river in the 16th century and who liked to promenade with his family by the river. The word 'bar' means riverside path. The area gradually fell into decline as the shallow depth of the Liffey forced the docks area eastwards and Temple Bar sank into decay, its dark alleys harbouring the poorest citizens of Ireland. In the late 1970s, the land was acquired by Ireland's state transport company CIE, which had plans to build a huge bus depot on the site. While plans were being discussed the company rented out some of the derelict properties to artists, musicians and artisans.

In the 1980s, the residents and artists formed a lobbying group and set about trying to save Temple Bar, fighting for the preservation of the buildings in the area. The Irish government supported the cause and an organization called Temple Bar Properties was created to coordinate and administer the project; their information centre opened in early 2004. The progress made in the 1990s was staggering. This is now the cultural centre of the

city and the place to go for shopping, socializing, eating and drinking. The public open-air spaces, such as Meeting House Square, showcase Irish artistic talent, be it art, music or juggling. Streets a little further afield have also been brought under the Temple Bar umbrella, such as Cow's Lane, with its design shops, which has been redeveloped and pedestrianized.

Temple Bar has been almost too successful for its own good – with party revellers spilling out from the bars and restaurants, the residents and corporation believed the area was losing its way and gaining a reputation for over-indulgence and drunken debauchery. It still gets a bit rowdy at the weekends for some, but during the day and weekday nights it's a great place to be. Among the principal arts venues are the Button Factory music centre (▶ 102), the National Photographic Archive, Gallery of Photography, Temple Bar Gallery and Studios, and The Ark (▶ 76).

www.templebar.ie

✚ 21J 🚉 Tara Street 🚌 Cross-city buses

Temple Bar Information Centre

✉ 12 East Essex Street, Temple Bar ☎ 677 2255

🕐 Mon–Fri 9–5:30 (also Jun–Sep Sat 10–6, Sun 12:30–4:30)

WAR MEMORIAL GARDENS

These gardens are well off the tourist track, on the southern bank of the River Liffey opposite Phoenix Park. They are dedicated to the memory of the 49,400 Irish soldiers who died in World War I. The names of all the soldiers are contained in the two granite book rooms at either end of the gardens. Designed by the celebrated architect Sir Edwin

Lutyens, this moving place is well worth a visit. With herbaceous borders, sunken rose gardens and extensive tree planting, the gardens are enjoyable at any time of year.

✚ 13J ✉ Islandbridge ☎ 677 0236 🕓 Mon–Fri 8–dusk, Sat–Sun 10–dusk 👆 Free 🚌 25, 25A, 51, 66, 66A, 66B, 69

WHITEFRIAR STREET CARMELITE CHURCH AND ST VALENTINE'S SHRINE

This church is run by the Carmelite order, which returned from abroad in 1827 to re-establish a church in the city. There had been a priory on the site when it was seized during the Reformation in the 16th century. One of the best-loved churches in Dublin, it contains the relics of St Valentine, the patron saint of lovers. Valentine died in Rome, but his remains were finally returned to his native Ireland in 1836 as a gift from Pope Gregory XVI, in recognition of the preaching of the Irish Carmelite John Spratt. The casket containing his bones is kept in a shrine to the right of the high altar, and couples come here to pray, with special blessing services held on the saint's feast day, 14 February. Note the unusual oak statue of the Virgin (Our Lady of Dublin), the only surviving wooden statue from the sacking of Ireland's monasteries during the Reformation.

✚ 21K ✉ 56 Aungier Street ☎ 475 8821
🕓 Mon, Wed–Fri 7:45–6, Tue 7:45am–9:15pm, Sat–Sun 7:45–7:30. Closed pm on public hols
👆 Free 🍴 Coffee shop (€) 🚉 Pearse
🚌 Cross-city buses

through Viking and medieval Dublin

From Dublin Castle (➤ 38–39) go up the hill and turn left into Castle Street. At the end, go left into Werburgh Street; St Werburgh's Church is on the left.

The 18th-century church, named after the King of Mercia's daughter, was built on late 12th-century foundations.

Continue down until you see St Patrick's Cathedral (➤ 52–53) on your right. Cross the road and pass the cathedral on your right. Turn right into Kevin Street Upper; on the right is the Garda Station, site of the Episcopal Palace of St Sepulchre. Bear right into St Patrick's Close, with its medieval horse trough.

There are great views on all sides of St Patrick's Cathedral.

Turn right up Patrick Street and head towards Christ Church Cathedral (➤ 36–37). Walk right around the perimeter of the cathedral and follow the cobbled lane at the back across into Cross Lane South; on the left is Dvblinia (➤ 84). Turn right into St Michael's Close and left into Cook Street. On your left is St Audoen's arch (1240), leading to St Audoen's churches (➤ 88). Continue and go right into Bridge Street Lower.

On the left is the Brazen Head (➤ 97), the oldest pub in Dublin.

At the bridge, the site of the first Viking crossing, turn right into Merchant's Quay and then second right into Fishamble Street.

Copper Alley, up the hill on the left (running through the Harding Hotel), was one of the earliest Viking streets.

Continue to the top and turn left into Lord Edward Street, which filters into Dame Street; opposite City Hall is the Queen of Tarts.

Distance 3km (2 miles)
Time 2 hours
Start point Dublin Castle, Dame Street ✚ 20J
End point City Hall, Dame Street ✚ 21J
Lunch Queen of Tarts (➤ 59)

HOTELS

Barnacles Temple Bar House (€)

Superior budget accommodation with en-suite bedrooms, many overlooking the cobbled streets of Temple Bar. Communal TV room, kitchen facilities and breakfast room.

✉ 19 Temple Lane South ☎ 671 6277; www.barnacles.ie 🚉 Tara Street
🚌 Cross-city buses

Clarence (€€€)

Originally built in 1852, this classic hotel in Temple Bar has a fabulous contemporary look, brought by U2's Bono and The Edge. The chic interior has soft suede and leather and stunning floral arrangements. Individually designed guest rooms are stylishly decorated with rich colours and have crisp white linen.

✉ 6–8 Wellington Quay ☎ 407 0800; www.theclarence.ie 🚉 Tara Street
🚌 Cross-city buses

Harding (€€)

Close to Temple Bar, opposite Christ Church Cathedral, the Harding has had a facelift. Roomy en-suite bedrooms have contemporary furniture and soft furnishings, and most modern facilities. The lively bar has music on some evenings and the Copper Alley Bistro is a welcome addition.

✉ Copper Alley, Fishamble Street ☎ 679 6500; www.hardinghotel.ie
🚌 Cross-city buses

Parliament Hotel (€€)

A well-placed, reasonably priced hotel opposite Dublin Castle and just around the corner from Temple Bar. Offers all the usual facilities, plus a good all-inclusive Irish breakfast. Check the website for special deals.

✉ Lord Edward Street ☎ 670 8777; www.regencyhotels.com 🚉 Tara Street
🚌 Cross-city buses

RESTAURANTS

Bad Ass Café (€€)
See page 58.

Brazen Head (€€)

Reputed to be the oldest bar in town, the Brazen Head has loads of old-world charm. The upstairs restaurant, with large dressers and stucco ceilings, offers Californian and modern Irish cooking. Downstairs there is a carvery at lunchtime (▶ 59).

✉ 20 Bridge Street Lower ☎ 679 5186 🕔 Lunch, dinner 🚌 51B, 78A

The Chameleon (€–€€)

Come here for a taste of Indonesia in the heart of Temple Bar. This restaurant excels in the Dutch-Indonesian *rijsttafel*, a selection of dishes served with rice – the fish version is particularly good.

✉ 1 Lower Fownes Street ☎ 671 0362 🕔 Tue–Sun dinner only (opens at 5pm) 🚈 Tara Street 🚌 Cross-city buses

Eden (€€)

See page 59.

Gallagher's Boxty House (€€)

Real Irish food, focused around boxty, the Irish potato pancake. The great atmosphere and country-style setting – and the food of course – are popular with visitors.

✉ 20–21 Temple Bar ☎ 677 2762 🕔 Lunch, dinner 🚈 Tara Street 🚌 Cross-city buses

Il Baccaro (€€)

Rustic trattoria set in the vaulted chambers of a cellar where a great atmosphere prevails. Authentic Italian food and fine Italian wines straight from the barrel.

✉ Diceman's Corner, Meeting House Square ☎ 671 4597 🕔 Dinner daily, lunch Thu–Sat 🚈 Tara Street 🚌 Cross-city buses

Juice (€)

Cool place for cool people looking for a healthy option. Mostly dedicated to juices and smoothies, and vegetarian food inspired by the cuisines of Japan, Mexico and the Caribbean.

✉ 73–83 South Great George's Street ☎ 475 7856 🕔 Lunch, dinner 🚈 Tara Street 🚌 Cross-city buses

Les Frères Jacques (€€€)

The emphasis at this stylish restaurant is on fish and seafood, but there are also delicious meat options. Courteous staff.

✉ 74 Dame Street ☎ 679 4555 🕐 Lunch Mon–Fri, dinner Mon–Sat
🚇 Tara Street 🚌 Cross-city buses

Lord Edward (€€€)

Dublin's oldest seafood restaurant is in traditional surroundings above a pub. Dedicated to simple but very tasty fish dishes and luscious desserts like meringue drizzled with *crème anglaise*.

✉ 23 Christchurch Place ☎ 454 2420 🕐 Lunch Mon–Fri, dinner Mon–Sat
🚌 Cross-city buses

Mermaid Café (€€)

Bright and airy hot spot with unfussy minimalist fittings. An eclectic menu of Irish fare offers tasty fun dishes, but the biggest lure is the house special, crab cakes.

✉ 69 Dame Street ☎ 670 8236 🕐 Lunch, dinner 🚇 Tara Street 🚌 Cross-city buses

Oliver St John Gogarty (€€)

There's a more formal restaurant on the first floor of this traditional Irish pub where you can eat such delights as a vast pot of mussels cooked in wine and Bailey's sauce, or a generous helping of Irish stew. Pub food is served downstairs with live Irish music.

✉ 58–59 Fleet Street ☎ 671 1822 🕐 Lunch, dinner; Sun dinner only
🚇 Tara Street 🚌 Cross-city buses

Queen of Tarts (€)

See page 59.

Tea Room at the Clarence (€€€)

Inside a prestigious hotel owned by the rock group U2, this is a magnet for Dublin's rich and famous. Exciting modern Irish food is served in a spacious, serene room with soaring ceilings.

✉ The Clarence, 6–8 Wellington Quay ☎ 407 0813 🕐 Closed Sat lunch
🚇 Tara Street 🚌 Cross-city buses

Yamamori Noodles (€€)

This Japanese noodle and sushi house has a cheerful and sociable atmosphere plus great food.

✉ 71–72 South Great George's Street ☎ 475 5001 ⏰ Lunch, dinner
🚇 Pearse 🚌 Cross-city buses

SHOPPING

ART AND ANTIQUES
Antiques Quarter

Georgian Irish furniture and silver embody fine craftsmanship. Francis Street is a focus of Dublin's antiques trade. Here you'll find shops selling elegant, good-quality antiques and bric-à-brac.

Graphic Studio Gallery

The oldest print gallery in Ireland, representing the works of more than 100 of Ireland's most well-known or emerging artists.

✉ Through The Arch, off Cope Street, Temple Bar ☎ 679 8021;
www.graphicstudiodublin.com 🚇 Tara Street 🚌 Cross-city buses

O'Sullivan Antiques

You'll find all sorts here, from mahogany furniture and garden statues to gilt mirrors and delicate glass.

✉ 43–44 Francis Street ☎ 454 1143; www.osullivanantiques.com
🚌 Cross-city buses

Timepiece Antique Clocks

Intriguing shop where antique clocks are painstakingly restored and sold. The majority are Irish long-case clocks.

✉ 57–58 Patrick Street ☎ 454 0774; www.timepieceantiqueclocks.com
🚌 Cross-city buses

FASHION
Smock

This tiny boutique creates a cosy atmosphere where you can try on the simple but slightly quirky women's clothing.

✉ 20–22 Essex Street West, Temple Bar ☎ 613 9000 🚇 Tara Street
🚌 Cross-city buses

FOOD AND DRINK
Meeting House Square Food Market
Every Saturday – except over Christmas – local traders turn out between 9:30 and 5 to sell their fare at this food-lovers' haven. Local Irish foods include cheeses, fresh oysters, home-made breads and quiches, cakes, jams and yogurts. People with a sweet tooth will enjoy the chocolates or freshly made waffles.

Gallic Kitchen
The smell draws you to this pâtisserie, selling freshly made potato cakes, quiches, pies and cakes, plus other tasty treats to take away. You can also buy their goods from the Temple Bar Food Market on Saturdays.

✉ 49 Francis Street ☎ 454 4912 🚌 Cross-city buses

IRISH CRAFTS AND DESIGN
Irish fashion designer John Rocha has brought Waterford Crystal up to date with his clean, minimalist designs. Beautiful objects in stone, wood, glass and other natural materials can be bought in contemporary and traditional designs. Jewellery lives on in the replicas of the Tara brooch, Claddagh rings and Celtic knots, mixing modern design with tradition.

Cow's Lane Market
For up-to-the-minute one-off designs from Ireland's young fashionistas take a look at the market in Cow's Lane, held every Saturday (10–5:30). Pieces on sale range from clothing for adults and children to jewellery, accessories and homeware.

✉ Cow's Lane, Temple Bar ☎ No phone 🚉 Tara Street 🚌 Cross-city buses

Temple Bar Trading Company
Among all the usual range of souvenirs from Ireland, including a selection of Guinness and Jameson memorabilia, you can find some interesting local art, books on Ireland and Irish music CDs in this shop, the 'official' Temple Bar merchandise outlet.

✉ 43–44 Temple Bar ☎ 670 3527; www.thetemplebarpubdublin.com
🚉 Tara Street 🚌 Cross-city buses

MUSIC
Claddagh Records
Traditional and folk music emporium selling just about every recording that is currently available.

✉ 2 Cecilia Street, Temple Bar ☎ 677 0262; www.claddaghrecords.com
🚉 Tara Street 🚌 Cross-city buses

Waltons
Irish musical instrument specialist with an amazing display of harps, *bodhráns*, whistles, pipes, flutes, mandolins and accordions.

✉ 69–70 South Great George's Street ☎ 475 0661; www.waltons.ie
🚉 Pearse 🚌 Cross-city buses

SECOND-HAND CLOTHING
Dublin has several vintage and second-hand clothing stores where you might discover a genuine treasure.

Eager Beaver (✉ 17 Crown Alley ☎ 677 3342) in Temple Bar specializes in next-to-new clothing.

Flip (✉ 3–4 Upper Fownes Street ☎ 671 4299), also in Temple Bar, is the place for trendy shoppers on the trail of second-hand jeans, baseball jackets and other items of Americana.

Jenny Vander (✉ 50 Drury Street ☎ 677 0406) sells luxury evening wear for that special occasion.

ENTERTAINMENT
THEATRES
Olympia Theatre
See page 69.

Project Arts Centre
This former print works is now a centre for young theatre groups staging experimental performances.

✉ 39 Essex Street East ☎ 888 9613; www.project.ie 🚉 Tara Street
🚌 Cross-city buses

LIVE MUSIC
Button Factory

A premier music venue staging music, dance, theatre and art performed by home-grown and international talent.

✉ Curved Street ☎ 670 9202; www.tbmc.ie 🚉 Tara Street
🚌 Cross-city buses

PUBS, CLUBS AND BARS
Brazen Head

See page 60.

Hogan's

Huge, fashionable hang-out packed with bright young things.

✉ 35 South Great George's Street ☎ 677 5904 🚌 Cross-city buses

The Long Hall

See page 60.

O'Shea's Merchant

Nobody can resist joining in with the traditional music and dance that takes place every night.

✉ 12 Lower Bridge Street ☎ 679 3797 🚌 51B, 78

Rí Rá

A diverse crowd immerse themselves in the sounds of a variety of music at this relaxed and fashionable club.

✉ Dame Court ☎ 671 1220; www.rira.ie 🚉 Tara Street 🚌 Cross-city buses

The Stag's Head

See page 61.

SPORT

HORSE RACING
Leopardstown Racecourse ✉ Leopardstown Road, Foxrock ☎ 284 0500
🚌 86, 118

The Curragh ✉ Co Kildare ☎ 045 441 205 🚌 Bus Éireann 126 (extra buses on race days) 🚉 Kildare to Newbridge

Southside East

Stately Georgian architecture, a cluster of outstanding national museums, a famous university and some of the best shopping in Ireland are all located in this area. There is so much to do and see in this relatively compact part of the city that just walking around and taking in all the colours, sounds and contrasts is quite an experience.

Grafton Street is the hub of the shopping area, a traditional (though pedestrianized) street scene, full of people and dotted with all kinds of street performers, with a glittering modern shopping centre at one end. Narrow side streets are a colourful mix of smaller shops, cafés and pubs, and surrounding streets have

interesting individual shops and classy designer boutiques. Nearby you can wander into the peaceful haven of Trinity College and discover the treasures of its old library, or visit the National Museum, Natural History Museum (closed for restoration) or National Gallery, next door to the parliament buildings of Leinster House. Further south is fine Georgian architecture concentrated around leafy Merrion and Fitzwilliam squares, and the lovely St Stephen's Green, an oasis of calm in the heart of the city. Take afternoon tea at the historic Shelbourne hotel to complete the central Dublin experience.

BALLSBRIDGE

This leafy suburb was laid out mainly in the mid-19th century but it still retains some grand Georgian houses, making it an exclusive and expensive place to live. It is sometimes known as the Embassy district, as foreign consulates have taken up residence here, along with smart hotels and the Royal Dublin Society Showgrounds, where prestigious events are held, such as the Dublin Horse Show. Close to the Lansdowne Road DART station is the Irish national rugby stadium, currently undergoing restoration.

🚊 27T 🖂 Southeast of city centre 🚉 Lansdowne Road 🚌 5, 7, 7A, 18, 45, 46, 84

BANK OF IRELAND

The bank began life as the upper and lower houses of the old Irish Parliament in 1739, the first purpose-built parliament buildings in Europe. The House of Commons was destroyed by fire in 1792,

but the House of Lords remains intact and can be visited. The Act of Union of 1800 shifted direct rule to London and the parliament buildings, on becoming vacant, were purchased by the Bank of Ireland in 1802. The House of Lords has a fine vaulted ceiling and oak panelling, a sparkling Waterford Crystal chandelier and huge tapestries depicting the 1689 siege at Londonderry and the 1690 battle of the Boyne. Original architect Edward Lovett Pearce designed the recessed south-facing piazza of Ionic columns and the rooms behind. James Gandon added the curving and windowless screen and the east-facing portico between 1785 and 1789.

✚ 22J ✉ 2 College Green ☎ 677 6801 ⏰ House of Lords: Mon, Tue, Fri 10–4, Wed 10:30–4, Thu 10–5. Bank of Ireland Arts Centre: Tue–Fri 10–4 ✋ Free; arts centre inexpensive 🚆 Tara Street 🚌 Cross-city buses

BEWLEY'S ORIENTAL CAFÉ

This café is a Dublin institution and worth visiting for the ambience alone. The family connection goes back to the 1840s when Joshua Bewley set up as a tea merchant. His son Ernest opened the first branch in South Great George's Street (now closed) in 1894. He introduced coffee and his wife baked scones and cakes. As the cafés grew in popularity, the family opened the now famous Grafton Street branch in 1927. Here you can sip coffee or eat a meal amid the original art-nouveau and art-deco features. This is where writers including Brendan Behan and Patrick Kavanagh came during the 1950s. On the second floor is the Café Theatre (call for details of performances) where you can watch live shows over a light lunch for €15. There are also evening events. Further branches of Bewley's can be found in Waterstones bookshops and a contemporary café in Dublin airport.

✚ 22K ✉ 78 Grafton Street ☎ 672 7720 ⏰ Mon–Thu 7:30am–11pm, Fri–Sat 7:30am–1am, Sun 8am–11pm; Mezz Café: daily 8am–midnight; Café Bar Deli: Thu–Sat noon–11, Sun–Wed noon–10; Café Theatre: Mon–Sat performances start 12:50pm 🚆 Tara Street 🚌 Cross-city buses

DUBLIN CITY LIBRARY AND ARCHIVE

Dublin City Library, re-opened in July 2003 after major renovations, offers all the usual facilities of a lending library, plus a business information facility and music library. Of most interest to visitors are the excellent Dublin City Archive and Dublin & Irish Local Studies Collections. These archives contain the records of Dublin's civic government since 1171 and give a vivid picture of the city over eight centuries. In the local studies section there is a fascinating collection of books, newspapers, photographs, maps, prints, theatre programmes, posters, ballad sheets and audio-visual material giving a unique insight into the city of Dublin. You can look through the local parish records and trace your family history if you have Irish ancestors, although the main centre of genealogical studies is at the National Library (► 114–115) in Kildare Street. There is also a 100-seat public reading room and a café.

www.dublincity.ie/living_in_the_city/libraries

🔳 25Q 📧 138–144 Pearse Street ☎ 674 4999 🕓 Mon–Thu 10–8, Fri–Sat 10–5 👜 Free 🚉 Pearse 🚌 2, 3

FITZWILLIAM SQUARE

This is one of Dublin's most famous squares. The first house was built here in 1714, which means the square's architecture spans the reigns of all four Georgian kings. The central garden is private and only the residents hold keys. The artist Jack B Yeats (1871–1957), who lived at No 18, is among the illustrious people to have resided here. There is plenty of Georgian detail, including original fanlights, and on some houses a box-shaped recess that held the lamps. Look, too, for original door knockers and elaborate iron foot-scrapers. Some houses have spikes set into the wall beside the windows, installed to deter 19th-century burglars, and

there are examples of ornamental iron balconies and attractive metal coal-hole covers.

🚩 23L 🤚 Free 🚌 Cross-city buses

GRAFTON STREET

Dublin's most popular thoroughfare is only 200m (650ft) long and 6m (20ft) wide. This attractive pedestrianized street, linking Trinity College and St Stephen's Green, is lined with four-storey Georgian buildings, and together with some of the smaller alleyways off the street, houses a selection of Dublin's best shops, restaurants, cafés – especially Bewley's (➤ 105) – pubs and bars. Flower sellers and street musicians add to this attractive city scene.

🚩 22K ✉ Grafton Street 🚊 Tara Street/Pearse 🚌 Cross-city buses

GRAND CANAL

Canals were the innovative form of cargo transport in the 18th century and Dublin's Grand Canal and Royal Canal were no exception. The Grand Canal crossed Leinster from Dublin to the River Shannon in Offaly, with a branch south to join the lovely River Barrow. Some 6km (4 miles) of the canal loops around Dublin, though it has carried no commercial traffic since the early 1960s. It's a pleasant place to stroll or take a boat trip, and is a haven for wildlife. At Grand Canal Quay, a few minutes' walk from the DART city station, is the Waterways Visitor Centre (currently closed for restoration), which houses an interactive multimedia exhibition of Ireland's inland waterways. It forms part of the quay's ambitious development project, which will include a new marina, theatre, apartments and offices. Grand Canal Square, at Grand Canal Dock between Sir John Rogerson's Quay and Pearse Street, is one of the largest paved public spaces in Dublin. Developed by the Dublin Docklands Development Authority, it is part of the revival of the north and south banks of the River Liffey, destined to be the key cultural focal point for the city. Cafés, shops and galleries have started trading and more are due in the ongoing phase of development. There is plenty of room for outdoor performances and festivals, with innovative lighting enhancing the space. The Grand Canal Theatre on the east side of the square, the work of world-renowned architect Daniel Libeskind, is due to open in 2009. A state-of-the-art performance arts centre, it will seat 2,000 people. A good two-hour walk along the towpath takes you all the way to Kilmainham. You can rest on the bench near Baggot Street Bridge, next to the bronze statue of poet Patrick Kavanagh (1905–67), who loved this stretch of water.

✚ 24M ✉ Grand Canal Quay 🚊 Grand Canal Dock 🚌 2, 3

IVEAGH HOUSE AND GARDENS

Iveagh House was donated to the state by Sir Robert Guinness, 2nd Earl of Iveagh, in 1939. Originally two houses when built in the 1760s, the Guinness family bought the properties in the 1860s and linked them under a stone façade, incorporating the family arms on the pediment. They subsequently altered the interior to include a new ballroom with an impressive domed ceiling. The house is now used by the Department of Foreign Affairs and is not open to the public. Hidden beyond Iveagh House are the lovely, secluded Iveagh Gardens. This is one of Dublin's finest but least well-known parks, just south of St Stephen's Green and entered by a small side street, Clonmel Street. Designed in 1863 by Ninian Niven, it includes a central area with lawns, statues and fountains echoing the Bois de Boulogne in Paris. Other areas have a more natural feel with a rustic grotto, woodlands and wilderness. There is also a maze and archery lawn reminiscent of Hampton Court in London. It's the perfect place to escape the hectic city on a warm summer's day. The gardens have become a popular venue for performances and festivals. The Taste of Dublin, a celebration of food and drink, is held here in mid-June, where you can sample the signature dishes supplied by some of the best chefs in the city. The Bud Light Revue comedy festival, which takes place over three days in late July, features more than 50 acts. Throughout the summer the gardens play host to jazz, theatre and dance. In July the National Concert Hall presents The Summer Proms in the Iveagh Gardens, a huge all-seater event.

🚌 22L ✉ Clonmel Street ☎ 475 7816 🕐 Mar–Oct Mon–Sat 8–6, Sun and public hols 10–6; Nov–Feb Mon–Sat 8–4, Sun and public hols 10–4 💶 Free 🚌 Cross-city buses

a walk around Dublin's pubs

Begin at the Stag's Head (▶ 61) in Dame Court, a small road off Dame Lane. Walk south to Exchequer Street and turn left. Continue to the Old Stand, one of Dublin's oldest pubs, on the left. Opposite, on the corner of Wicklow Street, is the International Bar. Turn right into William Street South and leave Powerscourt Shopping Centre on your left; opposite is Grogan's.

Grogan's has long been popular with writers and artists.

Continue towards the end of the street, turning left into Chatham Row and into Chatham Street; Victorian-style Neary's is on your right. Turn left into Grafton Street and next left into Harry Street for McDaid's (▶ 60). Return to Grafton Street and go straight across to Anne Street South; halfway down is the John Kehoe (▶ 132).

Kehoe's is an excellent example of a traditional old-style pub with plenty of *craic*.

Continue along Anne Street South and turn left into Dawson Street; take the next left into Duke Street to Davy Byrnes (▶ 60), a former haunt of James Joyce. Continue on and turn right into Grafton Street; take the second left into Suffolk Street. Follow the road round into Church Lane where you will find O'Neill's, a popular student watering hole, on the corner. Follow the road round and turn left into Dame Street. Cross the road and take the first right into Anglesea Street. At the end is the Oliver St John Gogarty (▶ 60) on the right and the Auld Dubliner on the left. Turn left into Temple Bar (▶ 91–92).

There are numerous pubs, bars and eating places here, including the Temple Bar, with its beer garden.

Distance 1.5km (1 mile)
Time Depends how thirsty you are
Start point Stag's Head, Dame Court ✚ 21J
End point The Temple Bar, 47–48 Temple Bar ✚ 21J
Lunch Good choice of pubs, restaurants and cafés in Temple Bar

LEINSTER HOUSE

This is one of Dublin's finest Georgian town houses, built in 1745 for the Earl of Kildare. It was renamed when the Earl became Duke of Leinster in 1766. The building eventually passed to the government and in 1922, with the forming of the Irish Free State, it became the headquarters of the new government. Today it is the seat of the Oireachtas (parliament) and houses the Dáil (lower house) and the Seanad (upper house or Senate).

✚ 23K ✉ Kildare Street ☎ 618 3781 🕐 Call for information ✋ Free 🚇 Pearse 🚌 Cross-city buses ❓ Visits by tour only, 2 hours

MERRION SQUARE

Languishing on a rock on the edge of Merrion Square's central park is a superb statue of Oscar Wilde. The author lived at No 1 between 1855 and 1876, and his house is a fine example of the city's Georgian architecture. Merrion is one of Dublin's most prestigious squares, laid out in 1762, and bordered by Leinster House, the National Gallery, the Natural History Museum and numerous smaller examples of Georgian splendour. Here you will find town houses with wrought-iron balconies, brightly painted doors, fanlights and elaborate door-knockers. The learned and the illustrious have lived here, including W B Yeats and the Duke of Wellington. Just off the square is Number Twenty Nine (➤ 117), a Georgian gem. The park is a delightful place to be on a sunny day, with its outstanding array of seasonal floral displays. Every summer Saturday and Sunday (10:30–6) there is an art exhibition.

✚ 24K ✉ Merrion Square 🕐 Park: daylight hours only 🚇 Pearse 🚌 Cross-city buses

NATIONAL GALLERY

Best places to see, ➤ 48–49.

NATIONAL LIBRARY

The library opened in 1890 in a late 19th-century Renaissance-style building, designed by Sir Thomas Deane. It was originally built to house the collection of the Royal Dublin Society, the institution concerned with the implementation of Dublin's national museums and galleries. The National Library contains the world's largest collection of Irish documentary material: books, manuscripts, newspapers, periodicals, drawings, photographs and maps. Its mission is to collect and preserve these documents and to make them available to the public. It does not lend them out and all research has to take place in the reading rooms. The domed reading room on the first floor is particularly magnificent, and

luminaries such as James Joyce worked here. You will need to get a reader's ticket to access any information, but it is free to look around. The library is most visited for its Genealogy Service (Mon–Fri 10–4:45, Sat 10–12:30) and family history research. There is a huge resource of Catholic parish records, 19th-century land valuations, trade and social directories, estate records and the largest collection of newspapers in Ireland, containing the all-important Births, Deaths and Marriages columns. The office of the Chief Herald and the Heraldic Museum (closed for restoration) are also within the library. The huge collection of the National Photographic Archive has now moved to Temple Bar (➤ 91–92). **www.**nli.ie

🗺 23K ✉ Kildare Street ☎ 603 0200 🕐 Mon–Wed 10–8:30, Thu–Fri 10–4:30, Sat 10–12:30 ✋ Free 🍽 Café (€) 🚊 Pearse 🚌 Cross-city buses

NATIONAL MUSEUM
Best places to see, ➤ 50–51.

NATIONAL PRINT MUSEUM
An idiosyncratic little museum in a former soldiers' chapel houses a unique collection of objects related to the printing industry in Ireland. Much of the machinery is still in full working order. Guided tours make this a much more fun experience than it sounds. The processes of printing, from Gutenburg's Bible of 1455 through to the political printed material of the Easter Rising of 1916, are documented and the various methods of production and bookbinding explained. The guides, some of them retired printers, are very knowledgeable. Upstairs the walls are adorned with newspapers, showing the different styles of printed presentation and recalling major historic events in Ireland.

🗺 27S ✉ Garrison Chapel, Beggar's Bush, Haddington Road ☎ 660 3770 🕐 Mon–Fri 9–5, Sat–Sun 2–5. Closed public hols. Some weekend opening, check for details ✋ Moderate 🍽 Coffee shop (€) 🚊 Grand Canal Dock 🚌 7, 7A, 45

NATURAL HISTORY MUSEUM

For an original Victorian experience look no further than Dublin's fascinating Natural History Museum. It may be known as the city's 'Dead Zoo', but it gives a unique insight into the way Victorians treated the study and display of animals, and the values that went with that. You won't find interactives or touch-screen technology here; instead you will find antique displays showing some 10,000 stuffed animals – drawn from a collection of around 2 million specimens. There are displays devoted to Irish animals, including skeletons of the huge, extinct Irish deer or elk, complete with impressive antlers, and animals, birds, fish, reptiles, insects and invertebrates from around the world. A huge 20m (65ft) long skeleton of a humpback whale is suspended from the ceiling and there is the skeleton of the fascinating but sadly extinct dodo. Unfortunately, the museum is currently closed for major restoration work until further notice.

www.museum.ie

✚ 23K ✉ Merrion Street ☎ 677 74444 ⏰ Check website for latest information ✋ Free 🚇 Pearse
🚌 Cross-city buses

NEWMAN HOUSE

This is in fact two houses, both of them among the finest Georgian houses in Dublin. Cardinal Newman used the mansion in the 1850s to launch his great experiment to bring education to the Catholic Masses. The Catholic University of Ireland was established here in 1865 and provided further education for men such as James Joyce and Eámon de Valera, who did not wish to attend the Protestant Trinity College. Newman House remains part of the original university, now known as University College Dublin. The houses are of interest for their spectacular plasterwork and superlative 18th-century interiors. Number 85 has examples of work by Switzerland's great Lafranchini brothers, who decorated the walls and ceilings.

➕ 22L ✉ 85–86 St Stephen's Green ☎ 716 7422 🕓 Jun–Aug Tue–Fri, tours at 12, 2, 3 and 4 ✋ Moderate 🚆 Pearse 🚌 Cross-city buses ❓ Guided tours only

NUMBER TWENTY NINE

Beautifully restored Number Twenty Nine is one of Dublin's Georgian jewels. It is laid out as the home of a middle-class family between 1790 and 1820, and offers a rare insight into the life of the period. An audio-visual show at the start of the tour introduces you to the family members, then leads from the servants' quarters in the basement to the attic playroom. Throughout are original artefacts and furnishings of the period, all recapturing the spirit of the age. It is the everyday items, in addition to some wonderful paintings, furnishings and plasterwork, that really bring this home to life.

➕ 25R ✉ 29 Fitzwilliam Street Lower ☎ 702 6165 🕓 Tue–Sat 10–5, Sun 1–5 ✋ Moderate 🍴 Tea room (€) 🚆 Pearse 🚌 7, 10, 45

OSCAR WILDE'S HOUSE

The home of writer Oscar Wilde from 1855 to 1876 is an excellent example of Georgian architecture. The restored house, on the north side of Merrion Square (➤ 113), with its remarkable cornices and architraves, was the first to be built on the square in 1762. In 1994 the American College Dublin took over the house and opened it for guided tours to groups of 25 or more, which must be reserved in advance. Renovation involved the revival of traditional crafts to repair the plasterwork and restore the original stone and wooden floors. Use of period paints, antique furnishings and reproduction Georgian furniture have given a first-class result.

➕ 24K ✉ 1 Merrion Square ☎ 662 0281 ✋ Moderate 🚉 Pearse
🚌 Cross-city buses

ROYAL COLLEGE OF SURGEONS

This internationally renowned institution is in one of the city's best Georgian buildings, overlooking St Stephen's Green (➤ 120). It dates from 1806 and has a neoclassical granite façade and distinctive round-headed windows. The three statues above the pediment are of Hygieia (goddess of health), Asclepius (god of medicine) and Athena (goddess of wisdom). The building was commandeered by Irish Volunteers under the leadership of Countess Markievicz in the 1916 Easter Rising, and you can still see the bullet marks on the façade.

➕ 22K ✉ 123 St Stephen's Green ☎ 402 2100 🚉 Pearse Street
🚌 Cross-city buses

ST ANN'S CHURCH

For the best view of this striking church, founded in 1707, look down Anne Street South from Grafton Street. The church was created for the rapidly evolving Georgian suburbs occupied by wealthy and influential residents. Its stunning Romanesque façade was added in 1868 by architects Deane and Woodward. Inside is a series of colourful stained-glass windows dating from the mid-19th century. It was here that the 18th-century nationalist leader Wolfe Tone was married in 1785, as was Bram Stoker, the author of *Dracula*, in 1878. St Ann's has a long tradition of charity work; in 1723 Baron Butler left a bequest to provide 120 loaves of bread each week for the poor, and today anyone may take a loaf from the shelf beside the altar.

✚ 22K 🖂 Dawson Street
☎ 676 7727 🕐 Mon–Fri 10–4 and Sunday service 🎫 Free
🚉 Pearse Street
🚌 Cross-city buses

ST STEPHEN'S GREEN

This pleasant park is one of the most famous in central Dublin. Once common ground where public hangings, whippings and burnings took place, today the 9ha (22-acre) green is a popular lunch-time venue for office and shop workers and a haven for visitors when sightseeing gets a bit too much. The duck pond, attractive flower beds and beautiful garden for the blind create a sanctuary from the city. The green was landscaped in the 18th century and St Stephen's became much sought after by the wealthy, who began to build their glorious Georgian town houses around the central park. Trees and paths, railings and gates were

installed and you could have access to the green at an annual cost of one guinea. The public were allowed free access again following an act of parliament proposed by Sir Arthur Guinness in 1877. The north side, known as Beaux Walk in the 18th-century, is still the most fashionable part, overlooked by the exclusive Shelbourne hotel (➤ 123). Highlights are the Fusiliers' Arch at the Grafton Street entrance, the Three Fates Fountain and the modern memorial, near Merrion Row, to the nationalist Wolfe Tone, better known locally as Tonehenge. Notable buildings around the green include the Royal College of Surgeons (➤ 118) and Newman House (➤ 117).

✚ 22L ✉ Top of Grafton Street ⏱ Mon–Sat 8–dusk, Sun, public hols 10–dusk ♿ Free 🚊 Pearse 🚌 Cross-city buses

TRINITY COLLEGE AND THE BOOK OF KELLS

Best places to see, ➤ 54–55.

UNIVERSITY CHURCH

It's easy to miss the front entrance to this church, which is next door to Newman House (➤ 117). Beyond the small entrance porch is a remarkable Byzantine-style interior. Commissioned by Cardinal Newman in 1856, the church was built on the garden plot between No 86 and No 87. The nave is richly decorated with Irish marble slabs and there is an ornate canopy over the altar. Look for the little birds on the capitals of the columns dividing the marble panels. John Hungerford Pollen, architect and friend of Newman, came over from England to supervise the building and also painted the elaborate ceiling. The church is lit by small windows set under the roof, and the atmosphere is one of tranquillity.

✚ 22L ✉ 87A St Stephen's Green ☎ 478 1606 ⏱ Mon–Sat 9–5:30, Sun 10–1, 5–6 ♿ Free 🚊 Pearse 🚌 Cross-city buses

HOTELS

Aston Hotel (€)

Aston Hotel provides a haven in contrast to the buzz of Temple Bar outside. Simple rooms with good use of pastel shades and pine furniture have a modern airy feel.

✉ 7–9 Aston Quay ☎ 677 9300; www.aston-hotel.com 🚉 Tara Street
🚌 Cross-city buses

Grafton Capital (€€)

Traditional Georgian town house well placed for Grafton Street and Dublin's cultural area. Spacious bedrooms are tastefully decorated and well equipped. Adjoining bar and restaurant.

✉ Stephen's Street Lower ☎ 648 1221; www.capital-hotels.com 🚉 Pearse
🚌 Cross-city buses

Harrington Hall (€€)

This beautifully restored Georgian guest-house beside St Stephen's Green offers the personal touch. Original Georgian features have been retained, along with all modern facilities. The bedrooms are furnished with elegant dark wood.

✉ 70 Harcourt Street ☎ 475 3497; www.harringtonhall.com
🚌 Cross-city buses

Merrion (€€€)

The epitome of grandeur in the heart of Georgian Dublin. Rooms are decorated in classic styles that reflect the 18th-century architecture and have opulent marble bathrooms. Renowned for its restaurant, Patrick Guilbaud (► 126). Pool, gym and spa.

✉ Merrion Street Upper ☎ 603 0600; www.merrionhotel.com 🚉 Pearse
🚌 Cross-city buses

Mespil (€€)

A warm and friendly welcome greets you at this modern hotel overlooking the Grand Canal. Stylish bedrooms offer a high level of comfort at good prices.

✉ Mespil Road ☎ 488 4600; www.leehotels.com 🚉 Grand Canal Dock
🚌 10

Morgan (€€)

A contemporary design based on uncluttered elegance, with clean simple lines. Bedrooms feature beechwood furniture, spacious bathrooms, ISDN lines, VCRs and CD players.

✉ 10 Fleet Street ☎ 643 7000; www.themorgan.com 🚆 Tara Street
🚌 Cross-city buses

Pembroke Townhouse (€€)

Excellent accommodation and service has won this 18th-century townhouse in Ballsbridge a loyal following. Individually decorated bedrooms merge modern style with Georgian elegance.

✉ 90 Pembroke Road ☎ 660 0277; www.pembroketownhouse.ie
🚆 Lansdowne Road 🚌 5, 7, 45

Shelbourne (€€€)

This much-loved hotel has a rich and historic past. The graceful Georgian building has been magnificently restored and boasts a stylish address overlooking St Stephen's Green.

✉ 27 St Stephen's Green ☎ 663 4500; www.marriott.com ☎ Pearse
🚌 Cross-city buses

RESTAURANTS

Avoca Cafés

Avoca Handweavers (➤ 159) have added award-winning cafés to their business empire. There are branches around the Dublin area at Kilmacanoge, Avoca Village, Powerscourt House and Suffolk Street. Famous for their home-made products, Avoca's innovative menus include Thai broth, confit of duck salad, beef stew and a selection of breads with various dips. They are legendary for their desserts and their excellent scones and biscuits.

Aya (€€)

A hip Japanese sushi bar furnished with minimalist wooden tables and chairs. Help yourself to the many delicacies as they glide past on the revolving conveyor belt. Seating for normal dining, too.

✉ Brown's Department Store, Clarendon Street ☎ 677 1544 🕐 Lunch, dinner 🚆 Pearse 🚌 Cross-city buses

Balzac (€€€)

Chef Paul Flynn heads up a great team producing fine, well-prepared food using first-class ingredients. This is *the* place to eat, in one of the finest dining rooms in the city.

✉ La Stampa Hotel, 35 Dawson Street ☎ 677 4444; www.lastampa.ie/balzac-restaurant ◉ Lunch, dinner Mon–Sat 12–3, 6–11, Sun 1–8 ▣ Pearse ▣ Cross-city buses

Bang Café (€€)

A hip clientele comes here for the buzz and the modern European menu. Try the signature dish of bangers and mash. Friendly staff.

✉ 11 Merrion Row ☎ 676 0898 ◉ Lunch, dinner. Closed Sun ▣ Pearse ▣ Cross-city buses

Bewley's Oriental Café (€)

See pages 58 and 105.

Brownes Brasserie (€€€)

A sophisticated dining-room in a Georgian town house. The classy fare is traditional Irish with a modern twist.

✉ 22 St Stephen's Green North ☎ 638 3939 ◉ Lunch Sun–Fri, dinner daily ▣ Pearse ▣ Cross-city buses

Café Java (€)

A popular breakfast and lunch-time haunt catering for all tastes – from bagels to poached eggs with bacon. You may have to wait.

✉ 5 Anne Street South ☎ 660 0675 ◉ Breakfast, lunch ▣ Pearse ▣ 11, 11A, 11B, 13, 46A

Café Mao (€€)

See page 59.

Cavistons (€€)

This small seafood restaurant serves wonderfully fresh, simply cooked fish that speaks for itself. Very popular so reserve a table.

✉ 59 Glasthule Road, Sandycove ☎ 280 9245 ◉ Lunch only. Closed Sun and Mon ▣ Sandycove/Glasthule ▣ 59

Cedar Tree (€€)

A delicious selection of Lebanese dishes and *meze (falafel*, spicy sausage) in a Middle Eastern ambience.

✉ 11 St Andrew's Street ☎ 677 2121 🕐 Dinner only 🚉 Pearse
🚌 Cross-city buses

Chili Club (€€)

This Thai restaurant is renowned for its tasty – and hot – curries and satays at reasonable prices. Cosy dining-room.

✉ 1 Anne's Lane, off Anne Street South ☎ 677 3721 🕐 Lunch Mon–Fri, dinner daily 🚉 Pearse 🚌 11, 11A, 11B, 13, 46A

Cornucopia (€)

Established, buffet-style vegetarian restaurant. The hot breakfast is a must, and the casseroles and vegetable quiches are good, too.

✉ 19 Wicklow Street ☎ 677 7585; www.cornucopia.ie 🕐 Breakfast, lunch, dinner Mon–Sat (Sun till 7) 🚉 Pearse 🚌 Cross-city buses

Dax (€€–€€€)

A welcome addition to the Dublin dining scene, Dax serves mainly Provençal dishes, cooked using local produce. Located in a town-house basement. Early Bird and tapas menus are good value.

✉ 23 Pembroke Street Upper ☎ 676 1494; www.dax.ie 🕐 Tue–Fri lunch, Tue–Sat dinner 🚌 11, 11a, 46; Luas Harcourt

Dunne & Crescenzi (€)

An Italian deli, wine shop and café. Seves the freshest deli-type dishes, such as authentic paninis made with buffalo mozzarella.

✉ 14 Frederick Street South ☎ 677 3815 🕐 Lunch, dinner 🚉 Pearse
🚌 Cross-city buses

Fitzer's (€€)

A popular restaurant chain offering relaxed dining. This one is a bright high-tech space with a fiery modern European menu. There are other branches at the National Gallery and in Temple Bar.

✉ 51 Dawson Street ☎ 677 1155; www.fitzers.ie 🕐 Lunch, dinner
🚉 Pearse 🚌 Cross-city buses

Jacob's Ladder (€€)

Formal restaurant with lovely views over the Trinity College playing fields. The imaginative modern Irish cuisine has a style of its own and is some of the best in Dublin.

✉ 4–5 Nassau Street ☎ 670 3865 🕐 Closed Sun, Mon 🚉 Pearse
🚌 Cross-city buses

L'Ecrivain (€€€)

Chef Derry Clarke conjures up his French-inspired modern Irish cuisine here. Heavenly dishes are complemented by excellent wines. Very expensive but worth every penny.

✉ 109a Baggot Street Lower ☎ 661 1919 🕐 Lunch Mon–Fri, dinner Mon–Sat 🚌 10A

Lobster Pot (€€€)

Delightfully old-fashioned restaurant with a nautical theme. First-class traditional cooking that specializes in fish.

✉ 9 Ballsbridge Terrace, Ballsbridge ☎ 668 0025 🕐 Closed Sat lunch and Sun 🚉 Lansdowne Road 🚌 5, 7, 7A, 45

Nude (€)

See page 59.

Patrick Guilbaud (€€€)

Beautifully cooked and presented dishes clearly show the flair and innovation of this French chef. The elegant dining-room has a fine collection of Irish art and the service is second to none.

✉ 21 Upper Merrion Street ☎ 676 4192; www.restaurantpatrickguilbaud.ie
🕐 Lunch, dinner Tue–Sat 🚉 Pearse 🚌 Cross-city buses

Roly's (€€)

This buzzing bistro is popular with the locals, which makes for a great atmosphere. Robust Irish dishes like pork stuffed with rhubarb and apple offer something different and the freshly baked speciality breads alone are worth the trip to Ballsbridge.

✉ 7 Ballsbridge Terrace, Ballsbridge ☎ 668 2611 🕐 Lunch, dinner
🚉 Lansdowne Road 🚌 5, 7, 7A, 45

Thornton's (€€€)

Thornton's has a reputation for exquisite cooking and this restaurant is arguably one of the best in Ireland. Innovative international cuisine includes signature dishes such as roast suckling pig with poi tin sauce.

✉ Fitzwilliam Hotel, 128 St Stephen's Green ☎ 478 7008 🕒 Closed Sun, Mon 🚇 Pearse 🚌 Cross-city buses

Unicorn (€€€)

Fashionable lunch spot where socialites gather to eat from the antipasto bar. In the evening there's a bistro-style menu of Italian classics served in a plain, unspoiled trattoria-style setting.

✉ 12B Merrion Court, off Merrion Row ☎ 676 2182 🕒 Lunch, dinner. Closed Sun 🚌 Cross-city buses

SHOPPING

ART AND ANTIQUES

Apollo Gallery

A collection of work by primarily Irish painters, plus some sculpture and prints.

✉ 51c Dawson Street ☎ 671 2609 🚇 Pearse 🚌 Cross-city buses

IB Jorgensen Fine Art

Expect to pay top prices at this exclusive gallery owned by Ireland's famous fashion designer. The fine art includes works by Jack Yeats, Mary Swanzy and Evie Hone.

✉ 29 Molesworth Street ☎ 661 9758 🚇 Pearse 🚌 Cross-city buses

John Farrington Antiques

The rich and famous visit this small shop filled with silver, glass, Irish furniture and the most sought-after items – antique jewellery.

✉ 32 Drury Street ☎ 679 1899 🚇 Pearse 🚌 Cross-city buses

Lemon Street Gallery

Work by a variety of international and Irish artists is showcased at this refreshing gallery, with a relaxed atmosphere.

✉ 24–26 City Quay ☎ 671 0244 🚇 Pearse 🚌 Cross-city buses

Silver Shop
The imaginative antique silver and silver-plate items sold here make an ideal special gift. Prices can be high.

✉ Second Floor, Powerscourt Townhouse Centre, William Street South
☎ 679 4147; www.silvershopdublin.com 🚇 Pearse 🚌 Cross-city buses

BOOKS AND MUSIC
Cathach Books
Antiquarian bookshop stocking Irish-interest books.

✉ 10 Duke Street ☎ 671 8676; www.rarebooks.ie 🚇 Pearse
🚌 Cross-city buses

Celtic Note
This small store sells music of all descriptions, from folk and traditional ballads to rock and contemporary.

✉ 12 Nassau Street ☎ 670 4157 🚇 Pearse 🚌 Cross-city buses

Hodges Figgis
Well-known bookstore spread across three floors. Its books cover all subjects, with an emphasis on Celtic and Irish culture.

✉ 56–58 Dawson Street ☎ 677 4754 🚇 Pearse 🚌 Cross-city buses

McCullough Pigott
Irish music enthusiasts can spend hours thumbing through the sheet music and gazing at the musical instruments here.

✉ 25 Suffolk Street ☎ 677 3188 🚇 Pearse 🚌 Cross-city buses

DEPARTMENT STORES AND SHOPPING MALLS
Avoca
Stocks its own range of innovative clothing, accessories, gifts and household items. Don't miss the food hall and café.

✉ 11–13 Suffolk Street ☎ 677 4215; www.avoca.ie 🚇 Pearse
🚌 Cross-city buses

Brown Thomas
Sophisticated store on Dublin's most fashionable shopping street showcasing designer clothes and other high-class goods such as

cosmetics, household items and lots more. Quite pricey, but look for the sales – you could find a bargain.

✉ 88–95 Grafton Street ☎ 605 6666 🚊 Pearse 🚌 Cross-city buses

Powerscourt Townhouse

Classy boutiques, high-quality handicraft and antiques shops, art galleries and restaurants surround the inner courtyard of an elegant converted 18th-century Georgian town house.

✉ 59 William Street South ☎ 671 7000; www.powerscourtcentre.com 🚊 Tara Street/Pearse 🚌 Cross-city buses

St Stephen's Green Centre

The three floors here house a mix of international chain stores and specialist shops. The top-floor café has fine views over the green.

✉ St Stephen's Green/top of Grafton Street ☎ 478 0888; www.ststephensgreen.com 🚊 Pearse 🚌 Cross-city buses

FASHION
Alias Tom

Everything you need to dress a man from head to foot by top international names such as Hugo Boss and Dublin-born designers like John Rocha. The staff are attentive without being intrusive.

✉ Duke House, Duke Lane ☎ 671 5443 🚊 Pearse 🚌 Cross-city buses

A Wear

This Irish main-street chain sells fashionable clothes and accessories at low prices, allowing you to follow the dictates of fashion without breaking the bank.

✉ 26 Grafton Street ☎ 872 4644 🚊 Pearse 🚌 Cross-city buses

Louise Kennedy

Hailed as Ireland's leading designer, Kennedy's tasteful clothing is sold alongside a crystal collection and luxury accessories, in a restored Georgian house that exudes style, just like her clothing.

✉ 56 Merrion Square ☎ 662 0056; www.louisekennedy.com 🚊 Pearse 🚌 Cross-city buses

FOOD AND DRINK

Avoca Food Hall

Packed with enticing produce such as oils, preserves, pastas and biscuits, all under the Avoca label.

✉ 11–13 Suffolk Street ☎ 677 4215 🚊 Pearse 🚌 Cross-city buses

Butlers Chocolates

Mrs Bailey-Butler's recipe for luxurious hand-made chocolates has been handed down through the generations since 1932.

✉ 51A Grafton Street ☎ 616 7004; www.butlerschocolates.com 🚊 Pearse
🚌 Cross-city buses

Celtic Whiskey Shop

Apart from having one of the best selections of Irish whiskies in the city, there are tempting hand-made Irish chocolates and an assortment of wines and liqueurs for sale.

✉ 27–28 Dawson Street ☎ 675 9744; www.celticwhiskeyshop.com
🚊 Pearse 🚌 Cross-city buses

Magills

Old-fashioned delicatessen filled with charcuterie (deli), traditional Irish cheeses and patés, smoked salmon, herbs and spices, and much more.

✉ 14 Clarendon Street ☎ 671 3830 🚊 Pearse Street
🚌 Cross-city buses

Mitchell & Son Wine Merchants

The oldest wine merchant in Dublin stocks unusual and exclusive vintages in the basement, along with all the usual brands.

✉ 21 Kildare Street ☎ 676 0766 🚊 Pearse 🚌 Cross-city buses

IRISH CRAFTS AND DESIGNS

Blarney Woollen Mills

Traditional hand-woven products from the Cork-based mills, plus tweeds, lace and linen, alongside names like Waterford Crystal.

✉ 21–23 Nassau Street ☎ 451 6111; www.blarney.com 🚊 Pearse
🚌 Cross-city buses

Cleo

This small shop, run by three generations of the Joyce family since 1936, sells authentic hand-knits and clothes made from traditional Irish natural fibres. Items are expensive but unique.

✉ 18 Kildare Street ☎ 676 1421 🚊 Pearse 🚌 Cross-city buses

House of Ireland

Quality craft shop geared towards tourists, stacked high with mainly woollen and tweed clothes made in Ireland. You can also buy cut crystal, fine china and other items that make ideal gifts.

✉ 38 Nassau Street ☎ 671 1111; www.houseofireland.com 🚊 Pearse 🚌 Cross-city buses

Kevin and Howlin

A family-run shop considered the best place to buy Donegal tweed clothing. The hardwearing items come in many patterns and styles.

✉ 31 Nassau Street ☎ 677 0257; www.kevinandhowlin.com 🚊 Pearse ☎ Cross-city buses

Kilkenny Centre

For stylish items made in Ireland, look no further. The amazing pottery, glassware, jewellery and fashion is creatively traditional.

✉ 6 Nassau Street ☎ 677 7066 🚊 Pearse 🚌 Cross-city buses

Louis Mulcahy

Sells the work of one of Ireland's most prolific potters. Here you can buy hand-thrown ceramics, plus lamps and tableware.

✉ 46 Dawson Street ☎ 670 9311; www.louismulcahy.com 🚊 Pearse 🚌 Cross-city buses

ENTERTAINMENT

CLUBS

Lillie's Bordello

You need to dress to impress to enter this trendy nightspot. Spot the celebrities among the beautiful people.

✉ Adam Court, Grafton Street ☎ 679 9204; www.lilliesbordello.ie 🚊 Pearse 🚌 Cross-city buses

POD

'Place of Dance' is a stylish, futuristic space, with the hottest DJs.

✉ Harcourt Street ☎ 476 3374; www.pod.ie 🚌 Cross-city buses

LIVE MUSIC
National Concert Hall

See page 68.

The Sugar Club

This cool, chic cocktail bar heats up to sounds ranging from jazz, Latin and blues to Indie rock and funk.

✉ 8 Lower Leeson Street ☎ 678 7188; www.thesugarclub.com 🚉 Pearse Street 🚌 10, 11, 14, 15, 44, 46, 86

PUBS AND BARS
Café en Seine

A trendy young crowd comes to this spectacular place to drink in extravagant style.

✉ 40 Dawson Street ☎ 677 4567 🚉 Pearse 🚌 Cross-city buses

Dawson Lounge

A tiny doorway and a narrow flight of steps lead to the smallest pub in Dublin – worth a look even if you don't stay for a pint.

✉ 25 Dawson Street ☎ 671 0311 🚉 Pearse 🚌 Cross-city buses

Doheny & Nesbitt

See page 60.

John Kehoe

The mahogany interior in this atmospheric pub has a wonderful Victorian bar where excellent beer is sold.

✉ 9 Anne Street South ☎ 677 8312 🚉 Pearse 🚌 Cross-city buses

The Bank

Stained-glass ceilings, hand-carved plasterwork, mosaic flooring – just as it was when the Belfast Bank opened here in 1895.

✉ 20–22 College Green ☎ 677 0677 🚇 Tara Street 🚌 Cross-city buses

Northside

Long overshadowed by the Southside, this part of the city has always had a unique character – more workaday and down to earth, but with such gems as the Dublin Writers Museum, the renowned Abbey and Gate theatres and, of course, the splendid central thoroughfare of O'Connell Street. Today, things are a little different north of the river, with the rejuvenation of the Smithfield and dockland areas bringing a trendy cachet to the whole scene.

O'Connell Street is still the hub, a wide street where shops, hotels and fast-food outlets are anchored by the impressive and historic General Post Office, famous for the role it played in the 1916 Easter Rising. Opposite the GPO is the soaring, slender Spire, erected in 2002. The southern end is presided over by a great statue of Daniel O'Connell, then comes O'Connell Bridge and the River Liffey. East along the river stands the imposing Custom House, while the quays to the west lead to the Four Courts, a superlative National Museum of Decorative Arts and History, housed in the former Collins Barracks, and the glorious Phoenix Park.

This is a fascinating part of the city to explore, with its mix of earthy street markets, lofty cultural establishments, trendy bars, statues and monuments, and parks and gardens.

ABBEY THEATRE

The Irish National Theatre was founded in 1903 by co-directors W B Yeats and Lady Augusta Gregory. Premises were purchased in Abbey Street and the new theatre was first opened to the public on 27 December, 1904. In its early days there were riots after performances of plays by playwrights such as Sean O'Casey. Following a fire in 1951, the Abbey remained closed until 1966. The Peacock Theatre was incorporated in the basement with the prime objective of showcasing new plays by burgeoning Irish writers. Established writers, including Brian Friel and Hugh Leonard, have their new works premièred

here, and classic plays from the European and world theatre, such as *The Playboy of the Western World* by J M Synge, are regularly produced. The Abbey is moving to a new home in the Docklands area in 2010.

www.abbeytheatre.ie
✚ 22H ✉ 26 Abbey Street Lower
☎ 878 7222 ⊗ Box office: Mon–Sat 10:30–7 ✋ Expensive, varies according to performance 🚉 Tara Street, Connolly 🚌 Cross-city buses; Luas Abbey Street

BLESSINGTON STREET BASIN

Now known as Dublin's 'secret garden', Blessington is only 10 minutes' walk from O'Connell Street. The Basin was originally constructed around 1803 to provide a reservoir for the city's water supply. In the 1860s it was used exclusively to provide water to

two distilleries – Jamesons in Bow Street and Powers in John's Lane – and this continued until the 1970s. The Basin was completely renovated in 1994 and is now a peaceful haven for visitors and local residents, and a safe environment for wildlife.

✚ 8E ✉ Blessington Street ☎ Dublin Parks 661 2369 ⏰ Dawn–dusk
✋ Free 🚌 10

THE BRAM STOKER DRACULA EXPERIENCE

Bram Stoker, author of the famous novel *Dracula* (1897), was born in the seaside suburb of Clontarf. This museum, dedicated to him, opened in 2003 at a cost of over €2 million. It covers an area of 929sq m (10,000sq ft) and makes use of all the latest technology. The 'Time Tunnel to Transylvania' transports you to the depths of Count Dracula's castle, to the Blood Laboratory and Renfield's Lunatic Asylum; not for the faint-hearted. There is also a section devoted to Stoker's life and his literary achievements. .

www.thebramstokerdraculaexperience.com

✚ 12E (off map) ✉ Westwood Club, Clontarf Road ☎ 805 7824 ⏰ Fri 4–10, Sat–Sun 12–10 ✋ Expensive 🍽 Restaurant, bar (€–€€) 🚏 Clontarf Road 🚌 27, 27B, 31, 32, 32A, 32B, 42, 42A, 42B, 43, 127, 129, 130

THE CASINO, MARINO

Although now surrounded by modern suburbia, the Casino ('small house') is one of the finest 18th-century neoclassical buildings in Ireland. George III's architect, Sir William Chambers, designed it along the lines of a Roman temple, and it contains 16 beautifully decorated rooms. It was built for James Caulfield, 1st Earl Charlemont, as a summer house where he could indulge his passion for all things Italian, following his Grand Tour of the Mediterranean. Throughout the rooms are fine ornamental plasterwork, exceptional parquet floors of rare woods, and practical features such as drainpipes hidden in ornate columns. The Casino was acquired by the state in 1930, after it had fallen into disrepair. Considerable restoration in the 1970s gradually returned it to its original condition, although work still continues.

✚ 12E (off map) ✉ Off Malahide Road, Marino ☎ 833 1618 🕓 Jun–Sep daily 10–6; May, Oct daily 10–5; Apr Sat–Sun 12–5; Feb, Mar, Nov, Dec Sat–Sun 12–4. Last admission 45 mins before closing ✋ Inexpensive 🚆 Clontarf Road 🚌 20, 20A, 27, 27B, 42, 42C, 123 ❓ Visit by guided tour

COLLINS BARRACKS

One of the most impressive museum spaces in Europe, the former barracks now houses the National Museum of Decorative Arts and History and is the administrative headquarters of the National Museum of Ireland. It was built as the Royal Barracks in 1704, and was renamed Collins Barracks in memory of Republican hero Michael Collins, following Irish independence. In 1994 the barracks were assigned to the National Museum of Ireland and after extensive restoration now display some of the 250,000 artefacts that make up exhibits charting Ireland's economic, social, political and military progress. There is an awesome collection of silver, ceramics, glassware, weapons, furniture and costumes. Highlights include the rare 14th-century Fonthill Vase, 19th-century neo-Celtic furniture and costume and jewellery in 'The Way We Wore' exhibition. Don't miss the 'Curators' Choice' – 25 objects chosen by the curators of the various collections. Further developments will include more temporary exhibition space and galleries for ethnography and earth sciences displays.

www.museum.ie

✚ 17H ✉ Benburb Street ☎ 677 7444 🕒 Tue–Sat 10–5, Sun 2–5 ✋ Free; guided tours inexpensive 🍴 Museum café (€) 🚌 25, 25A, 66, 67, 90; Luas Heuston

CUSTOM HOUSE

The best view of this impressive Georgian building, just past Eden Quay, is from the south side of the River Liffey; particularly at night when it lights up the skyline. The huge neoclassical Custom House – 114m (375ft) long – was designed by James Gandon in 1791 as the port of Dublin became increasingly more important to the city. The Act of Union of 1800 put paid to this as the custom and excise business moved to London and its role became redundant. Stretching along the waterfront, the main façade is made up of arched arcades with a Doric portico at its centre. It is topped by a green copper cupola or dome 38m (125ft) high with a 5m (16ft) statue of Commerce crowning the dome. Look for the frieze above the centre for a series of 14 allegorical heads that represent the 13 rivers of Ireland and the Atlantic Ocean. Other statues represent the four continents, while those of cattle emphasize Dublin's beef trade. The building suffered fire damage during one of the more dramatic events of 1921, although it was not completely destroyed, and restoration took place after the fire and again in the 1980s. Its bright Portland stone was cleaned recently. The building now contains government offices and is closed to the public.

✚ 23H ✉ Custom House Quay
☎ 888 2538 🚇 Tara Street
🚌 Cross-city buses

DUBLIN CITY GALLERY THE HUGH LANE

Charlemont House in Parnell Square is the perfect setting for the fine collection of modern art bequeathed to the nation by Sir Hugh Lane (1875–1915). He started his career as an apprentice art restorer and later became a successful London art dealer. He drowned when the *Lusitania* sank in 1915. The collection includes work by Monet, Degas and Renoir, as well as by 20th-century Irish artists such as Yeats and Orpen, and modern European artists including Beuys and Albers.

www.hughlane.ie

🕂 9E 🖂 Charlemont House, Parnell Square North ☎ 874 1903 🕒 Tue–Thu 10–6, Fri–Sat 10–5, Sun 11–5 ✋ Free 🍴 Café (€) 🚉 Tara Street/Connolly 🚌 Cross-city buses ❓ Guided tours by prior arrangement

DUBLIN WRITERS MUSEUM

The journalist and author Maurice Gorham (1902–75) was the first to propose the idea of this museum to Dublin Tourism. It was not, however, until 1991 that the museum finally came to fruition. Ireland has produced a staggering number of the world's greatest writers and where better to showcase their work than in this glorious 18th-century town house in central Dublin. The aim of the museum is to promote interest in Irish literature and, through its association with the Irish Writers' Centre next door, to encourage today's writers. The town house accommodates the museum rooms, library, gallery and offices, while an annexe behind houses the coffee shop, bookshop, and exhibition and lecture rooms.

Take the audio commentary that leads you through the displays, giving you the background story to Dublin's literary heritage. Displays include letters, manuscripts, paintings and personal

belongings and memorabilia. The museum also has a room
devoted to children's literature, and hosts regular readings and
temporary exhibitions. Take a little time to view the building itself,
with its exceptional stucco plasterwork and sumptuous
furnishings.

www.writersmuseum.com

✚ 9E ✉ 18 Parnell Square North ☎ 872 2077 🕐 Jun–Aug Mon–Fri 10–6,
Sat 10–5, Sun 11–5; Sep–May Mon–Sat 10–5, Sun and public hols 11–5
✋ Expensive 🍴 Café (€; closed Sun and public hols) 🚆 Connolly 🚌 Cross-
city buses ❓ Self-guided audio tour (30 mins); combined ticket available with
James Joyce Centre (➤ 177) and Shaw's Birthplace (➤ 89)

DUBLIN ZOO

Set in a beautifully landscaped area of Phoenix Park (➤ 149),
Dublin Zoo covers some 26ha (64 acres). It was founded in 1830
with animals from London Zoo. The aim of the zoo has changed
since its early days, when the objective was to show people,
who had never seen the like before, as many different species as
possible. Today the zoo is concerned with conservation, education

and animal study and it is part of an important international programme to breed and preserve endangered species, in particular the golden lion tamarin and the Moluccan cockatoo. One of the latest additions has been the African Plains, consisting of a large lake, pasture land and mature woodland. The animals featured on the plain include giraffes, hippos, rhinos, chimpanzees, lions, cheetahs and ostriches. Take the Nakuru Safari, a 25-minute tour of the African Plains, with full on-board commentary. Other highlights are the World of Cats, the Fringes of the Arctic and the City Farm, where children can handle pets and farm animals.

www.dublinzoo.ie

➕ 2F ✉ Phoenix Park ☎ 474 8900 ⏱ Mar–Oct Mon–Sat 9:30–6, Sun 10:30–6; Nov–Feb Mon–Sat 9:30–dusk, Sun 10:30–dusk. Last admission one hour before closing. Nakuru Safari daily between 11 and 4 ✋ Expensive; Nakuru Safari extra, moderate 🍴 Restaurant, cafés (€), picnic areas 🚌 10, 10A, 25, 26, 66, 66A, 66B, 67, 67A; Luas Heuston

FOUR COURTS

Four Courts was built by James Gandon between 1786 and 1802. This huge Georgian complex along the river is still Ireland's main criminal court so you can visit only when court is in session, although you cannot enter the courts and restricted areas. The building suffered damage during the Civil War and was not restored until the 1930s.

➕ 19H ✉ Inns Quay ☎ 872 5555 ⏱ Mon–Fri 10–1, 2–4 only when court is in session ✋ Free 🚌 Cross-city buses; Luas Four Courts

GAA MUSEUM

The GAA Museum in Croke Park is the home of the
Gaelic Athletic Association (GAA), the governing body
of Ireland's national sports – essentially hurling and
Gaelic football. The Irish are passionate about these
sports and about the stadium, which can hold 82,000
spectators and is always full to capacity for the
All-Ireland finals. The museum traces the history of
the sports through interactive touch screens and
sporting memorabilia, and highlights the personalities
involved in the sports over the years. A tour of the
stadium (Mon–Sat on the hour 10–3, Sun 1, 2 and
3pm) includes a look behind the scenes as well as
an opportunity to see the pitch.

www.museum.gaa.ie

➕ 11D ✉ Croke Park, St Joseph's Avenue ☎ 819 2323
🕐 Mon–Sat 9:30–5, Sun and public hols 12–5 (not open match
days) 💶 Tours: expensive 🍴 Coffee shop (€) 🚌 3, 11, 16

GATE THEATRE

Established in 1928, the Gate is housed in an elegant
late-Georgian building. From the outset it offered
Dublin audiences the best of international productions,
as well as plays from the classic and contemporary
Irish repertoire. Many famous names first performed
at the Gate, including James Mason and a young
Orson Welles. It also presents festivals of works by
playwrights such as Harold Pinter and Samuel
Beckett. Check the website for latest productions.

www.gate-theatre.ie

➕ 9F ✉ 1 Cavendish Row, Parnell Square East
☎ 874 4085; box office 874 4045 🕐 Check for performance
times; box office: Mon–Sat 10–7:30 💶 Depends on
performance 🚌 Cross-city buses

GENERAL POST OFFICE
Best places to see, ▶ 40–41.

GLASNEVIN CEMETERY
This cemetery was established in 1832 by Daniel O'Connell when Catholics were at last legally allowed to conduct funerals. It is Ireland's largest cemetery (49ha/121 acres), and around 1.2 million people are buried here. There are ornately carved Celtic crosses, Gothic mausoleums and tombs of the famous. Join one of the free tours to discover who has been buried here in the last two centuries. The names are synonymous with Dublin and Ireland, both political and cultural. Charles Stewart Parnell, Michael Collins and Eámon de Valera – the latter a leader of the 1916 Easter Rising, who went on to be Taoiseach seven times and president of Ireland twice – are among the famous political names. W B Yeats, Brendan Behan, the poet Gerard Manley Hopkins and the arts benefactor Alfred Chester Beatty lie here too. O'Connell is commemorated by a 51m (167ft) tall round tower. The paupers' graves are poignant reminders of the devastation wrought by famine and cholera in the 1840s.

www.glasnevin-cemetry.ie

✚ 6A ✉ Finglas Road, Glasnevin ☎ 830 1133
🕐 Mon–Sat 8:30–4:30, Sun 9–4:30 💵 Free
🚉 Drumcondra 🚌 40, 40A, 40B, 40C, 134
❓ Tours Wed, Fri 2:30; approx 2 hours

a walk in the footsteps of Joyce

From the James Joyce Centre (► 44–45) in North Great George's Street walk down the street and cross over Parnell Street into Marlborough Street. Go past St Mary's Pro-Cathedral on the right. Take the second right into Earl Street North, where you will find a statue of Joyce. Turn left into O'Connell Street. Cross over, and as you pass the General Post Office (► 40–41) take the second right into Middle Abbey Street.

Outside Eason's bookshop (No 78–79) you will find the first of 14 bronze plaques in the pavement, marking the route taken by Leopold Bloom, hero of Joyce's novel *Ulysses*. Take time to read the quotes on the plaques.

Retrace your steps to O'Connell Street and turn right; there's another plaque outside No 49. Continue over the bridge.

On the corner of Aston Quay and Westmoreland Street is the Royal Liverpool Assurance building, with a plaque outside.

Cross over Westmoreland Street. On the left at No 29, formerly Harrison's bakery, is another plaque. Continue until you come to the traffic island with a statue of Thomas More and a further plaque. Continue with Trinity College to your left, up Grafton Street and take the third left into Duke Street.

On the right is Davy Byrne's pub, a haunt of both Joyce and his fictional hero Bloom.

Continue and turn right at the end into Dawson Street, taking the next left into Molesworth Street. Look for a plaque on the left. Cross into Kildare Street and the final plaque is across the road outside the old entrance to the National Museum (▶ 50–51).

Distance 2km (1.2 miles)
Time 1.5 hours, more including stops
Start point James Joyce Centre, 35 North Great George's Street
➕ 10E
End point National Museum, Kildare Street ➕ 23K
Lunch National Museum café, Kildare Street (€) ☎ 677 7444

JAMES JOYCE CENTRE

Best places to see, ➤ 44–45.

KING'S INNS

The Honourable Society of King's Inns was founded in 1541 and is the oldest centre of legal training in Ireland. The present King's Inns building is a magnificent Georgian structure begun in 1800 by the illustrious architect James Gandon, who was responsible for the splendid Custom House (➤ 138) and Four Courts (➤ 141). The building was finally completed in the 1830s.

✚ 8F ✉ Henrietta Street ☎ 874 4840 🖐 Tours (by appointment only) expensive 🚌 83

NATIONAL BOTANIC GARDENS

To the north of the city, near Glasnevin Cemetery, are these botanic gardens, which opened in 1795. Apart from being a delightful place to stroll, they are also Ireland's premier centre for botany and horticulture. At the heart of the gardens are the beautifully restored Victorian glass and cast-iron curvilinear buildings, including the impressive Palm House. These glasshouses contain plants from across the world, including bamboo, banana and orchids. Outside, there is a rare handkerchief tree from China. In the Aquatic House you will find a variety of spectacular Amazonian water lilies. The 20ha (50-acre) park has around 20,000 different species of flora. Particular highlights include an arboretum, rock garden, rose gardens, yew tree walk, the glorious herbaceous borders and a rare example of Victorian carpet bedding. An education and visitor centre opened in 2000 to give people further insight into the extensive and important work of the botanic gardens.

✚ 7A ✉ Glasnevin ☎ 837 7596 🕔 Summer, Mon–Sat 9–6, Sun 10–6; winter, daily 10–4:30. Glasshouses and Alpine House restricted hours 🖐 Free; fee for parking 🚌 13, 19, 134 🚆 Drumcondra ❓ Guided tours available by prior arrangement (inexpensive)

O'CONNELL STREET

O'Connell Street became Dublin's main thoroughfare in 1794 when O'Connell Bridge was built. The bridge is one of the busiest crossings over the River Liffey, and is unique in Europe for being the only traffic bridge as wide as it is long. Highlights on the street include the General Post Office (➤ 40–41) and Dublin's famous department store, Clery's (➤ 153). A statue of Daniel O'Connell overlooks the bridge. You can still see bullet marks from the fighting in 1916. O'Connell Street has had a much needed facelift and one of its newest attractions is The Spire (also known as the Monument of Light, ➤ 151), erected in 2002.

✚ 22G ✉ O'Connell Street 🚆 Tara Street 🚌 Cross-city buses

OLD JAMESON DISTILLERY

This former distillery is in Smithfield Village (▶ 151), at the centre of the development of a once run-down area. The guided tour traces the history of Irish whiskey with exhibits and an audio-visual presentation. Whiskey was produced here from 1780 until 1971; it is now made in Middleton, Co Cork. Learn everything there is to know about Irish whiskey and how it differs from Scotch whisky, and don't miss the free dram in the Jameson Bar at the end of the tour. There is a huge choice of whiskey products for sale in the distillery shop.

www.oldjamesondistillery.com

✚ 19H ✉ Bow Street, Smithfield ☎ 807 2355 ◴ Daily 9:30–6 (last tour at 5:30) 🖐 Expensive 🍴 Restaurant, bar (€–€€) 🚌 68, 69, 79, 90; Luas Smithfield ❓ Gift shop

PARNELL SQUARE

Laid out in 1755, this is the city's oldest Georgian square after St Stephen's Green (▶ 120). Today it is a shadow of its former glory, but it has many points of interest, including the Gate Theatre (▶ 142) and the Garden of Remembrance (open during daylight). This peaceful garden is dedicated to those who gave their lives for Irish independence. The focal point is the bronze *Children of Lír* sculpture by Oisín Kelly. Other highlights are the Dublin Writers Museum (▶ 139), the Hugh Lane Gallery (▶ 139) and the 1758 Rotunda Hospital, the oldest maternity hospital in the world.

✚ 9F ✉ Parnell Square 🚆 Tara Street/Connolly 🚌 Cross-city buses

PHOENIX PARK

Phoenix Park is one of the largest city parks in Europe, if not the world, covering some 696ha (1,720 acres), and is encircled by a 13km (8-mile) wall. It was created in 1663 by King Charles II to provide a deer park. In 1745 it opened to the public and has been popular ever since. Ireland's tallest monument (63m/206ft), commemorating the Duke of Wellington's victory at Waterloo in 1815, can be found here. There's a lively historical interpretation of the park at the visitor centre and a children's exhibition on forest wildlife.

Adjoining the centre is Ashtown Castle, a medieval tower house. On the northern side of the park is Áras an Uachtaráin, the official residence of the president of Ireland, built in the Palladian style in 1751 (guided tours every Saturday). The rest of the park, with its tree-lined avenues woodland, lakes and gardens, is a great place to stroll, spot the wild fallow deer and watch the world go by.

🚲 1E 🚌 37, 38, 39; Luas Heuston

Phoenix Park Visitor Centre

✉ Phoenix Park ☎ 611 0095 🕐 Park open daylight hours. Visitor centre: Apr–Sep daily 10–6; mid- to end Mar 10–5:30; Oct 10–5; Nov to mid-Mar Wed–Sun 10–5 💶 Park free; visitor centre inexpensive 🍴 Restaurant and café (€€–€) ❓ Free tickets for tours of Áras an Uachtaráin available at visitor centre

ST ANNE'S PARK

St Anne's Park was once the home of the Guinness family. The grounds were acquired by Dublin Corporation in 1939, and the house was finally demolished in 1968. The park consists of extensive woodlands, hidden walled gardens, a mile-long avenue of stately oaks that originally led up to the house, and the famous rose garden. This glorious park is best viewed between June and September. There are also many sporting facilities, including football pitches, tennis courts and a 12-hole golf course.

12E (off map) Clontarf/Raheny Summer, daily 9–7; winter, 10–dusk Free Killester 130

ST MICHAN'S CHURCH

This church hides a grim secret in its crypt. The dry atmosphere caused bodies to mummify rather than decompose and, although the old coffins deteriorated and split open over time, the bodies remained intact, complete with hair and skin. A guided tour will show you this gruesome sight, with stories of those buried here, including the leaders of the 1798 rebellion, and barristers John and Henry Sheares. You can also see Wolfe Tone's death mask. The origins of the church can be traced back to 1095, although the current building was constructed in 1686. Inside highlights include

an organ believed to have been played by Handel and attractive woodcarvings of fruits and musical instruments above the choir.

✚ 19H ✉ Church Street ☎ 872 4154
🕐 Mar–Oct Mon–Fri 10–12:45, 2–4:45, Sat 10–12:45; Nov–Feb Mon–Fri 12:30–3:30
✋ Moderate 🚌 83; Luas Smithfield
❓ Access to vaults by tour only

SMITHFIELD

It's still all happening at Smithfield, the once run-down corner of the city. Redevelopment of the old cattle market began in the early 1990s and continues. Central to the 'village' is the Old Jameson Distillery (► 148), no longer in production but running tours and selling whiskey-related merchandise. Towering over the whole area is the 56m-high (184ft) Chimney, built in 1895. You can take a ride to the top for panoramic views over Dublin. Duck Lane, with its restaurant and interior design shops, opens onto a new cobbled plaza featuring floodlights and overhead gas heaters. Apartment blocks dominate the area and retail spaces are gradually beginning to fill up.

✚ 19H ✉ Smithfield Village 🚌 83; Luas Smithfield

THE SPIRE

The Spire, also known as the Monument of Light, stands across the road from the General Post Office on the site where Nelson's Column used to be. Made of light reflective stainless steel, it is 120m (394ft) high, 3m (10ft) in diameter at the base and only 15cm (6in) at the top. It rises majestically above the rooftops where it sways gently (but safely) in the breeze. It is central to the rejuvenation of this somewhat down-at-heel area.

✚ 22H ✉ O'Connell Street 🚆 Tara Street 🚌 Cross-city buses

HOTELS

Gresham (€€€)

Dublin's oldest hotel has undergone a transformation to provide a bright, more modern look – but the attentive staff remain the same. Bedrooms combine traditional style with modern comfort.

✉ 23 Upper O'Connell Street ☎ 874 6881; www.gresham-hotels.com
🚉 Connolly 🚌 Cross-city buses

Morrison (€€€)

Wood, stone and natural fabrics combine with vibrant colours to create a luxurious feel at this visually stunning boutique hotel by Irish designer John Rocha, overlooking the River Liffey.

✉ Lower Ormond Quay ☎ 887 2400; www.morrisonhotel.ie 🚉 Tara Street
🚌 Cross-city buses

RESTAURANTS

Chapter One (€€)

In the basement beneath the Dublin Writers Museum, the dining-room has pictures of Irish writers on the granite walls. Organic produce is used in the modern Irish cooking. Seared scallops and fennel, and loin of venison may be on the regularly changing menu.

✉ 18–19 Parnell Square ☎ 873 2266 🕙 Lunch Tue–Fri, dinner Tue–Sat
🚉 Connolly 🚌 Cross-city buses

Cobalt Café (€)

An ideal spot for a quick snack; the light menu at this bright and airy café offers generously filled sandwiches and cakes. Arty types come here to see the display of original paintings on the walls.

✉ 16 North Great George's Street ☎ 873 0313 🕙 Mon–Sat 10–5. Closed
Sun 🚉 Connolly 🚌 Cross-city buses

Halo (€€€)

Minimalist in style, this chic restaurant is in a striking atrium. The modern European fusion cooking includes divine dishes along the lines of pan-fried sea bass with a barigoule and champagne sauce.

✉ Morrison Hotel, Ormond Quay Lower ☎ 887 2400 🕙 Lunch and dinner
daily, breakfast Sat–Sun 🚉 Tara Street 🚌 Cross-city buses

The Harbourmaster (€€)

Located within the old harbourmaster's office, this atmospheric bar has a modern dining room serving contemporary food.

✉ Custom House Dock ☎ 670 1688; www.harbourmaster.ie ⏰ Daily lunch and dinner 🚆 Connolly 🚊 Luas Connolly

Rhodes D7 (€€–€€€)

Restaurateur Gary Rhodes' first Irish venture. A modern European menu uses the best Irish produce, served in spacious surroundings.

✉ The Capel Building, Mary's Abbey ☎ 804 4444; www.rhodesd7.com ⏰ Tue–Sat lunch and dinner, Sun–Mon lunch only 🚊 Luas Jervis

SHOPPING

BOOKS

Dublin Writers Museum Bookshop

In a city famous for its literary connections, it is appropriate that this excellent bookshop is inside the Dublin Writers Museum.

✉ 18–19 Parnell Street North ☎ 872 2077 🚌 Cross-city buses

Eason's

Vast general bookstore, with several branches, carrying a variety of books, magazines, art supplies and music. Also has a café.

✉ 40 O'Connell Street ☎ 858 3800; www.easons.ie 🚆 Tara Street/Connolly 🚌 Cross-city buses

DEPARTMENT STORES

Arnotts

Huge department store stocking everything from clothes and cosmetics to home entertainment, furnishings and sports gear.

✉ 12 Henry Street ☎ 805 0400; www.arnotts.ie 🚆 Connolly/Tara Street 🚌 Cross-city buses

Clery's

There is a huge range of goods, but it is ideal for Irish gifts. Known for its theatrical window displays and the gold-embossed clock.

✉ 18–27 O'Connell Street Lower ☎ 878 6000; www.clerys.ie 🚆 Tara Street/Connolly 🚌 Cross-city buses

ILAC Centre

Dublin's oldest shopping mall has had a face-lift and houses a Dunnes department store. Also bargain outlets and clothes stores.

✉ Henry Street ☎ 704 1460 🚇 Connolly/Tara Street 🚌 Cross-city buses; Luas Jervis

Jervis Centre

You will find most British main-street chains at this modern shopping complex on several floors. Huge top-floor food court.

✉ Henry Street ☎ 878 1323; www.jervis.ie 🚇 Connolly/Tara Street 🚌 Cross-city buses; Luas Jervis

FOOD AND DRINK
Old Jameson Distilley

The shop at the distillery (➤ 148) sells a range of Irish whiskey-flavoured items – cakes, truffles, jams, fudge and marmalade.

✉ Bow Street ☎ 807 2355 🚌 83; Luas Smithfield

STREET MARKETS

Moore Street Market, off Henry Street, is the most authentic market and is famous as the spiritual home of Molly Malone. Open daily, it is primarily a fruit and vegetable market.

ENTERTAINMENT

THEATRES
Abbey Theatre

See pages 68 and 134.

Gate Theatre

See pages 68 and 142.

CINEMAS
Cineworld

This huge centre has a cinema with 17 screens, simulated rides, computer games, themed bars and restaurants.

✉ Parnell Centre, Parnell Street ☎ 872 8444; www.cineworld.ie 🚇 Connolly 🚌 Cross-city buses

Savoy
An old-fashioned movie theatre with six wide screens and Dolby sound systems. It also hosts premières of Irish films.
✉ O'Connell Street ☎ 0818 776 776; www.savoy.ie 🚌 Cross-city buses

LIVE MUSIC
The Helix
This stunning state-of-the-art complex has three performance venues for classical music, drama and mainstream rock and pop.
✉ Dublin City University, Collins Avenue, Glasnevin ☎ 700 7000
🚌 13A, 19A, 103, 105

The Point
See page 69.

CLUBS
Spirit
Dance to soul, reggae, house and more – or chill out in the Virtue Room to serene sounds and holistic treatments.
✉ 57 Middle Abbey Street ☎ 877 9999; www.spiritdublin.com 🚆 Tara Street 🚌 Luas Abbey Street

The Vaults
Under Connolly station the 10 vaults house a restaurant, four bars and a nightclub. Call or check the website for what's playing.
✉ ISFC, under Connolly Station ☎ 605 4700; www.thevaults.ie 🚆 Connolly 🚌 Luas Connolly

SPORT
GAELIC GAMES
Gaelic football and hurling are played all over Co Dublin and the All-Ireland finals take place before sell-out crowds in early and late September. These fast and furious games are promoted by the Gaelic Athletic Association based at Croke Park, where there is a museum (➤ 142) devoted to Ireland's national games.
✉ Croke Park Stadium, St Joseph's Avenue ☎ 836 3222 🚌 3, 11, 11A, 16, 16A

Excursions

From fine country houses and gardens to prehistoric tombs, from mountains, lakes and valleys to splendid golf courses – there is something for everyone in the eastern counties around Dublin. The pace of life is slower than in the city and you will need a car to visit the more remote areas, but many of the main attractions can be reached by public transport. To the southwest are the rolling green fields of Co Kildare, an area famous for horse breeding and its racecourse, the Curragh. South are the wild peaks of the Wicklow Mountains, where there are great opportunities for walking and touring. To the north the extraordinary ancient burial sites at Brú Na Bóinne dominate Co Meath and further north in Co Louth is the site of the famous Battle of the Boyne of 1690.

AVOCA HANDWEAVERS

Located in the heart of Co Wicklow, in the village of Avoca, the handweavers began spinning and weaving blankets and clothing in 1723. The business, however, did not really flourish until the 1920s, when the Wynne sisters inherited the mill and with flair and ingenuity built an excellent venture marketing tweeds all over the world, supplying top-class designers and selling to royalty. It expanded with the introduction of rugs and throws using natural fibres, including lambswool and cashmere in a brilliant range of colours. You can visit the mill to see production in progress and hopefully pick up a bargain in the factory shop. The village has another claim to fame – it was the location for the popular BBC television drama *Ballykissangel*.
www.avoca.ie

✉ Old Mill, Avoca, Co Wicklow ☎ 0402 35105 ⏰ Daily 9–6 (9:30–5:30 in winter) 🚶 Free 🚌 Bus Éireann 133 to Avoca (service infrequent)

BECTIVE ABBEY

The original abbey was built in 1147 by Murchad, King of Meath. Little of the early building survives and what you can see in a field

by the River Boyne is really the ruin of a 15th-century fortified building – more castle than monastery. The abbey was repressed in 1536 and fell into disrepair. What remains gives an indication of a religious, defensive and domestic building. The religious aspects are the cloisters – the best-preserved part of the building – the nave and the chapter house. The defensive parts can be seen in the square tower and the domestic parts in the remains of fireplaces, chimneys and windows.

✉ Bective, Navan, Co Meath ☎ 046 943 7227 ⏰ Daily, daylight hours 🚶 Free 🚌 Bus Éireann service 109 Dublin to Navan, then 135 Navan to Scurloughstown stops at Bective Cross

BOOTERSTOWN BIRD SANCTUARY

Booterstown Marsh is the only bird sanctuary in South Dublin Bay, an important feeding and roosting area for ducks, geese and waders. As part of the bay, Booterstown Marsh is an essential stop-over and refuelling place for migrating birds. There are both freshwater and saltwater habitats and the birds include moorhen, teal, snipe, oystercatchers and Brent geese. Plant life is abundant too, and the protected saltmarsh grass is among the species that thrive here. During the 19th century most of the marsh was used for cultivation or grazing but was drained and subsequently used for gardens. After World War II, when it fell into disuse, the marsh vegetation gradually reclaimed the arable land, now administered by the National Trust for Ireland.

✉ Booterstown, Co Dublin ☎ The National Trust for Ireland 454 1786 🕓 Dawn–dusk 🚉 Booterstown

BRAY

This former refined Victorian seaside resort has become a playground for families and day-trippers. The safe sand and shingle beach stretches for 1.5km (1 mile) and can get very crowded in summer. You might prefer to walk along the cliffs at Bray Head, which, at 241m (790ft) above the sea, offer great views. On the seafront is the fascinating conservation-conscious National Sea Life Centre (▶ 77). Other activities in Bray include golf, sailing and fishing. Alternatively you can just wander along the esplanade that stretches from Bray Harbour to Bray Head and watch the world go by.

Just outside the town, at the foot of the Little Sugar Loaf mountain, is beautiful **Killruddery House and Gardens.** The house was originally built in the 17th century, but was remodelled in Elizabethan style in the 1820s. There are carvings by Grinling Gibbons and furniture by Chippendale, and a lovely orangery, added in 1852, has remarkable marble statues. The superb gardens were created in the 1680s in the French style.

🚉 Bray 🚌 45, 84

ℹ️ Old Courthouse, Main Street Bray, Co Wicklow ☎ 286 7128

Killruddery House and Gardens

✉️ Bray ☎ 286 3405; www.killruddery.com 🕐 Gardens: May–Sep daily 1–5, Apr weekends only; house: May, Jun, Sep daily 1–5 ✋ House and garden: expensive; garden only: moderate 🚉 Bray, then Finnegan bus stops close to entrance 🚌 84 from Dublin stops at Woodlands Hotel, then short walk to entrance

BRÚ NA BÓINNE

The Boyne Valley is strewn with some of Ireland's most important archaeological monuments. Brú Na Bóinne (Palace of the Boyne) has Europe's richest concentration of ancient monuments, including forts, henges, standing stones and the mysterious grand passage tombs of Newgrange, Knowth and Dowth. To understand the significance of the site you need to realize that these monuments are 1,000 years older than England's Stonehenge and 100 years older than the pyramids of Giza in Egypt. The River Boyne valley was first settled during the Stone Age and many other legends surround the site. Access to the monument is through the visitor centre only – from where you can gain background information before embarking on a tour. In high summer you should reserve places well in advance as the tours are restricted by numbers.

Newgrange

Newgrange was probably built more than 5,000 years ago by skilled builders. This is evident from the excellent condition of the tombs. The spectacular passage grave here is the high point of a visit. Built into a giant mound 85m (280ft) across and 10m (33ft) high, its perimeter is defined by nearly a hundred massive kerbstones (curbstones). The exterior is faced with brilliant white quartzite. At least 200,000 tons of stone went into its construction, with stones as large as 16 tonnes each brought from as far away as Co Wicklow. At the entrance to the tomb one of these kerbstones is marked with the distinctive spiral details of this area and above it is a rectangular opening like a mail box. It is through this roof box that the dawn light enters at the winter solstice and shines through to the interior. A lottery system gives people the chance to witness this event, otherwise you will have to make do with with a simulated experience. A guide leads you by torchlight along the 19m-long (62ft) passage into the heart of the mound and to the burial chamber, with its intricate corbelled ceiling rising

6m (20ft) above you. Here is the most amazing spiral abstract carved detail in the walls. When the tomb was excavated only a few bodies were found, unusual considering the tomb's size. It is possible that remains were removed regularly.

Knowth

You can see the great tomb of Knowth from the road, but you can access it only by taking a tour. This mound is defined by some 120

kerbstones and is surrounded by at least 17 small passage graves. Inside the main tomb (closed to visitors) are two passages and the stonework is rich with spiral and line carvings. The exterior is also beautifully decorated.

Dowth

Dowth contains some of the finest rock carvings anywhere in Ireland. It can be viewed from the road to the east of Newgrange. The passage grave here was heavily excavated by the Victorians and became popular with souvenir hunters.

✉ Donore, Co Meath ☎ 041 988 0300 🕐 Mar–Apr daily 9:30–5:30; May daily 9–6:30; Jun to mid-Sep daily 9–7; mid-Sep to end Sep daily 9–6:30; Oct daily 9:30–5; Nov–Feb daily 9:30–5. Knowth open: Easter–Oct only ✋ Varies according to site; visitor centre only: inexpensive 🍴 Tea room at visitor centre (€) 🚌 Bus Éireann 100 Dublin to Drogheda, then 163 to Donore village (10-min walk) ❓ Access to monuments by tour only, lasting 1 hour 15 mins (allow at least 3 hours if visiting both Newgrange and Knowth). Last tour departs 1 hour 45 mins before centre closes but it's best to visit early as it is often overcrowded and visitors are regularly turned away

CASTLETOWN HOUSE

This striking house was built in the Palladian style between 1722 and 1732 for the Speaker of the Irish Parliament and at the time Ireland's richest man, William Connolly. From humble beginnings, Connolly amassed his wealth by buying and selling forfeited property in the aftermath of the Battle of the Boyne in 1690. Castletown's opulent interior has elaborate rococo stucco work and a Long Gallery decorated in the Pompeian style of the 1770s. Look for the huge painting called *The Boar Hunt* by Paul de Vos (1569–1679) in the main hall. Connolly did not see the project through and died before the house was completed; his widow continued improvements. Her main contribution was Connolly's Folly, an unusual obelisk structure some 40m (130ft) high, 3km (2 miles) north of the house. The magnificent interiors of the house were subsequently completed by Lady Louisa Connolly, wife of William Connolly's great nephew, who moved here in 1759. One fascinating room is the Print Room, lined with elaborately framed prints from 18th-century magazines.

www.castletown.ie

✉ Celbridge, Co Kildare ☎ 628 8252 🕓 Easter to mid-Nov Tue–Sun 10–6
🖑 Moderate 🍴 Café/restaurant (€) 🚌 67, 67A ❓ Guided tour only, lasts approximately 45 mins

DALKEY

South of the city is the pretty seaside village of Dalkey, once called the 'town of seven castles'. Only two of these fortified houses now remain, standing opposite each other in the main street. Goat Castle remains totally intact and houses the **Heritage Centre,** with displays on the once important port. The view of the sea and mountains from the battlements is splendid. In summer you can visit Dalkey Island by boat, just a short distance offshore.

Dalkey Castle and Heritage Centre

✉ Castle Street, Dalkey ☎ 285 8366; www.dalkeycastle.com 🕓 Mon–Fri 9:30–5, Sat–Sun and public hols 11–5 🖑 Moderate 🚈 Dalkey

DOLLYMOUNT STRAND

Only 20 minutes from the city centre, Dollymount Strand is a 3km (2-mile) beach, a perfect place for walking, paddling or flying a kite. Nearby North Bull Island, a 300ha (741-acre) island formed after the construction of the Bull Wall (a North Sea wall) in the 1820s, is an important nature reserve and bird sanctuary with some 25,000 wading birds visiting in winter. You can drive on to the expanse of sand via a bridge at the west end and a causeway in the middle. An interpretative centre opens in summer (daily 10–4:30) to help with the identification of wildlife. There are splendid views across the bay to the Wicklow Mountains.

✉ North Bull Island, Causeway Road, off James Larking Road
👋 Free 🚆 Clontarf Road 20 mins
🚌 130

DROGHEDA

The town of Drogheda stands at the lowest bridging point of the River Boyne, just a few kilometres from the site of the famous Battle of the Boyne in 1690. It was first established by Viking traders in 911 and was an important Norman port in the 14th century. Little remains of the town walls but there are still elements of medieval architecture in the hilly streets, including St Lawrence's Gate, a fine four-floor barbican (tower). Also of interest is the Magdalene Tower, the only remains of the original Dominican friary of 1224. Above the south bank of the river – accessed from the riverside by steep steps – is the Norman motte (castle mound), topped by a Martello tower (c1808), with splendid views over the town. It is also the site of the **Millmount Museum,** housed in the old barracks, with exhibits relating to the town and its industries, an authentic 19th-century kitchen and a craft centre showcasing Irish design, including jewellery, knitwear and ceramics.

🚌 Bus Éireann service 163 to Drogheda 🚆 Drogheda
ℹ️ Mayorality Street, Drogheda, Co Louth
☎ 041 983 7070

Millmount Museum
✉️ Millmount Square, Drogheda, Co Louth ☎ 041 983 3097; www.millmount.net 🕐 Mon–Sat 9:30–5:30, Sun and public hols 2–5 🖐 Moderate

DUN LAOGHAIRE AND THE NATIONAL MARITIME MUSEUM

Dun Laoghaire (pronounced 'Dun Leary') has a fine harbour and is known as a seaside resort and a thriving port where car ferries from Holyhead on the Isle of Anglesey in Wales dock. From a small fishing village in the early 19th century, the town is now a thriving community and a popular place for the people of Dublin to visit on weekends. There's plenty to do, with lots of pubs and restaurants, water sports, boat trips around the bay and fishing, plus excellent walking and views along the coast. The **National Maritime Museum** in the Mariner's Church has displays of model boats and Irish naval memorabilia. Take a look at the *Great Eastern* display – the largest ship in the world when it was built in 1857. The display has a clockwork model of the ship, more than 100 years old.

🚊 Dun Laoghaire 🚌 7, 7A, 46A, 746

National Maritime Museum

✉ High Terrace, Dun Laoghaire ☎ 280 0969 🕐 Closed for renovation
💷 Free (donations welcome)

GLENDALOUGH

Deep in the heart of the Wicklow Mountains are the atmospheric remains of a remarkable monastic settlement founded in the 6th century by St Kevin, who came from one of Leinster's ruling families. He was abbot of Glendalough until his death in AD618 and the monastery became famous throughout Europe as a seat of learning. It remained an important place of pilgrimage well into the 18th century. The site is one of Ireland's premier attractions and can get very busy in high summer; the best time to visit is a quiet spring or autumn evening. The setting is magnificent, with the lake and the mountains making a superb backdrop, and the area is particularly popular with walkers. The ruins incorporate a 12th-century round tower and 11th-century St Kevin's Church, known as St Kevin's Kitchen. The roofless cathedral of St Peter and St Paul dates from the 12th century and is the largest ruin. There are several other churches and monastic buildings around the site, as well as numerous gravestones and crosses. Some of the remains, although visible from the shore, are accessible only by boat, including the Tempull na Skellig or 'church on the rock' and St Kevin's Bed, a small cave reputed to have been the saint's retreat. The visitor centre, also the information centre for the Wicklow Mountains National Park (➤ 180), has an audio-visual presentation to the site, and its interactive displays give a good insight into the life and times of St Kevin and the monastery.

🚌 St Kevin's bus twice daily from Dublin

Visitor Centre

✉ Glendalough, Bray, Co Wicklow ☎ 0404 45325 ◑ Mid-Mar to mid-Oct daily 9:30–6; mid-Oct to mid-Mar daily 9:30–5 ✋ Inexpensive ❓ Guided tour on request, 30–40 mins

HILL OF TARA

At first sight it may seem as if you are looking at a few grassy
humps and depressions in the landscape, but it is worth the trip,
not just for the superb views, but for the sense of history and
mythology evoked by this important neolithic place. Tara was
the main religious and political centre of Ireland during the
first millennium AD, where priests and kings would gather. It
remained the seat of the High Kings until the 6th century;
although its connection to royalty remained until the 11th century,
its importance was waning by this time with the spread of
Christianity. Among the more impressive remains is the Mound
of Hostages, a passage grave that, on excavation, revealed 40
Bronze Age cremations from around 2000BC. One of the most
prominent earthworks is the Royal Enclosure with a ring fort
known as Cormac's House in the centre. Here stands a pillar,
called Lia Faíl, or Stone of Destiny, where the High Kings

of Ireland were crowned. There is a visitor centre on site in St Patrick's Church, with an audio-visual display and tours of the site.

✉ Near Navan, Co Meath ☎ 046 90 25903 ⏰ Main site open during daylight hours May to mid-Sep. Visitor centre in St Patrick's Church mid-May to mid-Sep daily 10–6 ♿ Inexpensive 🍴 Café near site (€) 🚌 Bus Éireann service 109 to Tara Cross (ask driver for stop) ❓ Guided tours, 35–40 mins

HOWTH

A pleasant ride north on the DART will take you to Howth, a major fishing centre and yachting harbour. Howth (rhymes with both) is a popular residential suburb whose steep streets run down to the sea. The DART station is near the harbour and close to all the waterside activity, bars, pubs and restaurants. You can take a boat trip to view the small rocky island, Ireland's Eye, with its resident puffin colony, Martello tower and 6th-century monastic ruins. Above the town are the remains of St Mary's Abbey and 1km (0.5 miles) to the west is Howth Castle and the **National Transport Museum.** The 16th-century castle is closed to the public but the gardens are famous for their rhododendrons and azaleas. Hidden away in a farmyard is the transport museum, with its unique collection of restored old trams, fire engines and vans. From Howth Head there are splendid views over Dublin Bay, and

an 8km (5-mile) path around the head makes a dramatic walk.

✉ Howth Head 🚉 Howth 🚌 31, 31B

National Transport Museum

✉ Heritage Depot, Howth Castle Demesne, Howth ☎ 832 0427; www.nationaltransportmuseum.org ⏰ Jun–Aug Mon–Sat 10–5; Sep–May Sat–Sun and public hols 2–5 ♿ Inexpensive

KELLS (CEANANNUS MOR)

You probably wouldn't visit the town of Kells if it wasn't for its connection with the famous book, and a visit to the heritage centre puts the Book of Kells and the monastery into historical context. A monastery was founded here in AD550, but it was not until the early 9th century that the monks came with their famous illuminated manuscript from Iona, fleeing the Viking raids. The work was completed in Kells and displays in the heritage centre allow you to view the pages on computer. The book is now in Dublin's Trinity College Library (➤ 54–55), but there are some good replicas here to view.

🚍 Bus Éireann service 109 to Kells

Kells Heritage Centre

✉ The Courthouse, Headfort Place, Kells, Co Meath ☎ 046 92 47840
🕐 May–Sep Mon–Sat 10–6, Sun and public hols 1:30–6; Oct–Apr Mon–Sat 10–5 💷 Moderate 🍴 Café (€)

KILDARE

Since Kildare got its bypass in 2003, the centre has become pleasantly quiet. In the old Market House is the tourist information office, and a heritage centre that traces the history of Kildare and its surroundings. The town is dominated by St Brigid's Cathedral, built on the site of a former 5th-century monastery. The original 10th-century tower survives and is an impressive 33m (108ft) high.

Co Kildare is horseracing country and the home of the famous racecourse, the Curragh. Just south of Kildare is Tully House and the **Irish National Stud,** which was founded in 1900 by Colonel William Hall-Walker; now a state-run stud, it breeds some of the most famous racehorses in the world. The best time to visit the stables is between February and July, when there can be as many as 300 foals. Tours of the stable blocks and paddocks are available and there is a Horse Museum illustrating the importance of horses and racing to the Irish. Look out for the skeleton of Arkle, one of the stud's most famous champion stallions.

The **Japanese Gardens** at Tully House, landscaped between 1906 and 1910, include an impressive array of plants, from mulberry and cherry trees to magnolias and bamboo. There is a tea house and a miniature village carved out of rock from Mount Fuji.

The garden symbolizes the journey of a soul from Birth to Eternity, finally coming to rest in the Garden of Peace and Contentment. Along the way the soul encounters the Hill of Learning, the Walk of Wisdom, the Hill of Ambition and the Bridge of Life.

Also at Tully House is **St Fiachra's Garden,** a millennium project that seeks to re-create a monastic island hermitage in honour of St Fiachra, the patron saint of gardeners. Its use of natural materials, such as rock and water, creates a sense of spirituality and calm. You can see a stone cave decorated in sparkling Waterford Crystal and the statue of St Fiachra holding a seed standing on a rock in the lake.

🚌 Bus Éireann service 126 to Kildare 🚆 Kildare

ℹ️ Market House, Market Square, Co Kildare ☎ 045 521240 🕐 Mon–Fri 10–1, 2–5

Irish National Stud/Japanese Gardens/St Fiachra's Garden

✉️ Tully, Kildare ☎ 045 521617; www.irish-national-stud.ie 🕐 Mid-Feb to mid-Nov daily 9:30–5 💰 Expensive (covers both gardens and National Stud) 🍴 Restaurant (€€) 🚆 Kildare, then shuttle bus (every 20 mins) to stud and gardens ❓ Guided tour of the National Stud, allow 35 mins

KILLINEY

A short trip south on the DART takes you to Killiney, the 'Dublin Riviera', where national and international celebrities have set up home. But you don't have to be wealthy to enjoy some of the best views of Dublin and the surrounding area. The climb to the top of Killiney Hill takes about 30 minutes and rewards with exceptional vistas. Down at Coliemore Harbour fishermen run boat trips in summer to nearby Dalkey Island, with its bird sanctuary.
✉ Killiney 🚉 Killiney

MALAHIDE

Just 13km (8 miles) north of Dublin, and easily reached by the DART, is Malahide. This attractive seaside village has become an increasingly desirable place for Dubliners to live, and its pubs, restaurants, chic shops and marina make it popular with visitors too. One of the highlights on the edge of the village is **Malahide Castle.** Set in 100ha (247 acres) of woodland, the castle was both a fortress and a private home for nearly 800 years; the Talbot family lived here continuously from 1188 until 1973.

It is an interesting mix of architectural styles, with its central medieval core, a three-level, 12th-century tower, 16th-century oak room and additional Georgian embellishments and furnishings. On organized tours you can see the Talbot family portraits, together with paintings loaned by the National Gallery. Keep an eye out for one of the many ghosts believed to haunt the castle. In a separate building in the grounds you will find the Fry Model Railway (➤ 76).

🚆 Malahide 🚌 42

Malahide Castle

✉ Malahide Castle Demense, Malahide ☎ 846 2184; www.malahidecastle.com 🕐 Apr–Sep Mon–Sat 10–5, Sun and public hols 10–6; Oct–Mar Mon–Sat 10–5, Sun and public hols 11–5 💷 Moderate 🍴 Restaurant (€€)

MONASTERBOICE

The ruins of the monastery of St Buite, one of the most famous monastic settlements in Ireland, lie in an attractive secluded spot north of Drogheda. Founded in the 6th century, the monastery remained at the height of importance for 600 years until it was superseded by the new Cistercian foundation, Mellifont Abbey. Highlights are the 10th-century roofless round tower and the wonderful set of three high crosses. The finest is Muiredach's Cross, with elaborate sculptural detail and an inscription that reads 'A prayer for Muiredach by whom was made this cross'.

✉ Near Drogheda, Co Louth 🕐 Always accessible 💷 Free

POWERSCOURT HOUSE AND GARDENS

Set amid the wild landscape of the Wicklow Mountains, Powerscourt is one of the most magnificent gardens, both formal and semi-natural, in Europe. The view from the terrace is unbeatable, with its sweeping vista and a backdrop of mountain peaks. The original house, built in the 1740s, was gutted by fire in 1974 and has been the subject of a careful restoration project. It now houses an exhibition on the history of Powerscourt. You can visit the former ballroom, and there is a gallery of craft and design shops and the Terrace Café. But it is for the gardens that most visitors come; laid out in the mid-18th century, they comprise great formal terraces that drop down towards lakes and fountains, statues and decorative ironwork. There are American, Japanese and Italian gardens, as well as charming walled gardens with rose beds and borders, and even a pets' cemetery. The leaflet provided

will give you a self-guided tour of the gardens. If time allows, check out the 121m-high (397ft) waterfall, Ireland's highest, 5km (3 miles) away but still on the Powerscourt Estate.

www.powerscourt.ie

✉ Powerscourt Estate, Enniskerry, Co Wicklow
☎ 204 6000 🕓 Daily 9:30–5:30. Waterfall: summer 9:30–7pm; winter 10:30–dusk
💷 Expensive for house and gardens; waterfall moderate; free to enter estate 🍴 Restaurant and café (€–€€) 🚌 44C 🚉 Bray, then 185 bus
❓ Garden centre on site

SANDYCOVE AND JAMES JOYCE TOWER

Just south of Dun Laoghaire is the affluent village and popular commuter suburb of Sandycove. It is named after a small sandy cove near the rocky point on which a Martello tower was built in 1804 to withstand a threatened invasion along this coastline by Napoleon. James Joyce stayed in the tower for a week and it features in the opening chapter of his famous novel *Ulysses*. It now houses a small museum of Joycean memorabilia, including a collection of letters, photographs, first and rare editions and personal possessions of the author, including his guitar and walking stick. If you fancy a swim, directly below the tower is the Forty Foot Pool (complete with changing areas), traditionally an all-male nude bathing pool, but now open to both sexes; swimming costumes permitted!

James Joyce Museum

✉ James Joyce Tower, Sandycove ☎ 280 9265 🕓 Mar–Oct Mon–Sat 10–1, 2–5, Sun and public hols 2–6 💷 Moderate 🚉 Sandycove 🚌 59 from Dun Laoghaire

SLANE

Despite suffering from heavy traffic congestion, the estate village of Slane is a pleasant place to visit, with its fine Georgian houses. To escape from the busy main street head up the winding lane to the Hill of Slane. From this spot, St Patrick is said to have lit a fire announcing the arrival of Christianity and heralding the end of the pagan Kings of Tara. Here are the remains of a church and college established in 1512. **Slane Castle,** to the west of the village, has been home to the Conynham family since the 18th century. The castle suffered a devastating fire in 1991 and after ten years of renovation reopened to the public in 2001. You can see the fine Gothic Ballroom with its plasterwork ceiling completed for the visit of George IV in 1821. The castle grounds were landscaped by Capability Brown. Now mostly used for conferences, weddings and concerts, Slane Castle has also served as a location for films and U2 recorded their album, *The Unforgettable Fire*, here in 1984.

Slane Castle

✉ Slane, Co Meath ☎ 041 988 4400; www.slanecastle.ie ⏱ Guided tours: 2 May–2 Aug Sun–Thu 12–5 ✋ Expensive 🚌 Bus Éireann service 177 to Slane

TRIM

Trim is a thriving town on the River Boyne, and was once the site of one of the oldest and largest religious settlements in Ireland. The town is dominated by the Anglo-Norman **Trim Castle,** which was built by Hugh de Lacy in 1173. It is the largest such castle in Ireland, enclosing a 1.2ha (3-acre) site. The castle has hardly been altered since the 13th century and still bears the scars of warfare. Visitors can access the 21m-high (69ft) keep and grounds on a guided tour. Scenes from the 1995 epic film *Braveheart* were shot here. Across the Boyne are the ruins of Sheep's Gate and the

Yellow Steeple – the belfry tower of the former St Mary's Augustinian Abbey dating from 1368 and the most prominent remains here. It rises dramatically from the quiet meadow, left undisturbed since the town developed on the opposite bank in the 18th century. Other ruins of note are the 13th-century Cathedral of St Peter and St Paul and the Hospital of John the Baptist. The visitor centre gives more insight into these medieval ruins in its exhibition, The Power and the Glory, a clever multimedia display that underlines the consequences of the Norman arrival in Ireland.

🚌 Bus Éireann service 111 to Trim

Trim Visitor Centre

✉ Castle Street, Trim, Co Meath ☎ 046 94 37227 🕐 Mon–Sat 9:30–5:30, Sun and public hols 12–5:30 ✋ Free; audio-visual moderate

Trim Castle

✉ Trim, Co Meath ☎ 046 94 38619 🕐 Easter–Oct daily 10–6; Nov–Easter weekends 10–5 ✋ Moderate including keep tour ❓ Guided tours only to keep, 45 mins

WICKLOW MOUNTAINS NATIONAL PARK

A dramatic, secluded area of high mountains, peaceful valleys and lakes on the doorstep of Dublin, this park covers some 20,000ha (49,420 acres) with Lugnaquilla its highest point at 943m (3,094ft). Two scenic passes cross the mountains from east to west – the Sally Gap on the spectacular old military road from Dublin to Laragh, and the Wicklow Gap to the south. Much of the lower mountain slopes are covered in woodland; some trees are believed to be old enough to have supplied the timber for Dublin's St Patrick's Cathedral and London's Palace of Westminster. In the western foothills, several valleys have been flooded to form the Pollaphuca Reservoir, also known as Blessington Lake. This provides Dublin with water and electricity, and you can take a boat trip on the water. Scattered throughout the park are ancient hillforts and stone circles, as well as monastic sites such as Glendalough (➤ 168–169). Also within the park is Powerscourt House and Gardens (➤ 176–177).

🚌 St Kevin's bus twice daily from Dublin

Information Office

✉ Upper Lough, Glendalough, Wicklow Mountains National Park, Co Wicklow ☎ 0404 45425; www.wicklownationalpark.ie 🕙 May–Sep, daily 10–5:30; Oct–Apr, weekends 10–dusk 🎟 Free

HOTELS

CO KILDARE
Killashee House (€€€)
Amid exquisite gardens and woodland, with magnificent views of
the Wicklow Mountains, this majestic Victorian manor house is
steeped in history and has elegant rooms decorated with antiques
and warm colours. Spa facilities. Turner Restaurant.
✉ Killashee Demesne, Naas ☎ 045 879 277; www.killasheehouse.com

CO LOUTH
Bellingham Castle Hotel (€€)
On the coast, in wonderful surroundings, this 17th-century castle
oozes old-world splendour. Modern facilities harmonize with
antiques and all rooms – decorated with bright hues – have
breathtaking views.
✉ Castlebellingham ☎ 042 937 2176; www.bellinghamcastle.com

CO MEATH
Conyngham Arms Hotel (€€)
In the heart of the picturesque village of Slane, this mid-19th-
century building has a distinctive stone façade. The cosy inside is
Victorian in style with four-poster beds. Also has a fine restaurant.
✉ Slane ☎ 041 988 4444; www.conynghamarms.com

Station House Hotel (€€€)
A former station house lovingly transformed in keeping with the
original 1860s stone building. Exquisite rooms have been created
with individual style.
✉ Kilmessan ☎ 046 902 5239; www.thestationhousehotel.com

CO WICKLOW
Glendalough Hotel (€€)
Victorian building nestled amid amazing mountain scenery within
the Wicklow Mountains National Park. Furnished with traditional
Irish pieces; most rooms have views of the surrounding hills.
✉ Glendalough ☎ 0404 45135; www.glendaloughhotel.com

RESTAURANTS

CO DUBLIN

Johnnie Fox's Pub (€)
Beams and an open fire set the scene at this 18th-century coaching inn, known for its superb seafood, especially the fresh mussels. Traditional music sessions are held nightly.
✉ Glencullen ☎ 295 5647; www.jfp.ie

Guinea Pig Fish Restaurant (€€€)
See page 59.

CO KILDARE

High Cross Inn (€)
Delightful roadside pub dating back to the 1870s; sheep roam freely outside. The inn has a reputation for its great traditional fare.
✉ Bolton Hill, Moone ☎ 05986 24112 🕓 Lunch, dinner

Moyglare Manor (€€€)
The candlelit dining room is a romantic setting to enjoy imaginative food prepared using fruit and vegetables from the hotel's gardens. Country-house cooking includes sophisticated traditional favourites.
✉ Maynooth ☎ 628 6351 🕓 Closed lunch Sat

CO LOUTH

Forge Gallery Restaurant (€€€)
This hospitable restaurant is a great setting for excellent food combining rustic European and New Irish cuisines.
✉ Collon ☎ 041 982 6272; www.forgegallery.ie 🕓 Lunch Tue–Sun, dinner Tue–Sat

CO WICKLOW

Roundwood Inn (€€)
Cosy inn – popular with hikers – complete with roaring log fires and wooden benches. The award-winning food, Irish with a German influence, is served in the bar and in the restaurant.
✉ Main Street, Roundwood ☎ 281 8107 🕓 Bar meals daily; restaurant lunch Sun, dinner Fri, Sat (more evenings when busy)

Sight Locator Index

This index relates to the maps on the covers. We have given map references to the main sights in the book. Some sights may not be plotted on the maps.

Index

Acknowledgements

The Automobile Association would like to thank the following photographers, companies and picture libraries for their assistance in the preparation of this book.

Abbreviations for the picture credits are as follows – (t) top; (b) bottom; (c) centre; (l) left; (r) right; (AA) AA World Travel Library

4l Bective Abbey, AA/C Jones; **4c** St Patrick's Day Parade, AA/S Day; **4r** Trinity College, AA/S Day; **5l** Howth Head, AA/M Short; **5c** O'Shea's Merchant Pub, AA/M Short; **5r** Malahide Castle, AA/Slide File; **6/7** Bective Abbey, AA/C Jones; **8/9** River Liffey, AA/S Whitehorne; **10bl** St Patrick's Day Parade, AA/S Day; **10br** pony and trap, AA/S Whitehorne; **10/11** Café Life, AA/M Short; **11** Georgian House, AA/S Whitehorne; **12** Boxty House, AA/M Short; **12/13** English Market, AA/S Hill; **13** Bread-cake, AA M Short; **14l** Old Jameson Distillery, AA/S Day; **14r** McDaids Bar, AA/L Blake; **15** Galway Oyster Festival, AA/S McBride; **16/17** Temple Bar pub, AA/S Day; **17t** Bewleys Café, AA/S Whitehorne; **17b** Millenium Walk, AA/S Day; **18l** Dart Train, AA/M Short; **18r** Regency Doorway, AA/W Voysey; **18/19** Fitzsimon's Inn, AA/S Day; **19** River Liffey, AA/S Whitehorne; **20/21** St Patrick's Day Parade, AA/S Day; **24** St Patrick's Day Parade, AA/S Day; **25** Dublin Marathon, AA/S Whitehorne; **26** Dart Train, AA/M Short; **27** Sealink Ferry, AA/M Short; **28** General Post Office, AA/S Day; **30** Green Post Box, AA/S Whitehorne; **31** Tourist Information Centre, AA/S Day; **34/35** Trinity College, AA/S Day; **36** Christ Church Cathedral casket, AA/S Day; **36/37t** Christ Church Cathedral, AA; **36/37b** Christ Church Cathedral crypt, AA/S Day; **38/39t** Dublin Castle int, AA/S Day; **38/39b** Dublin Castle ext, AA/S Day; **39** Chester Beatty Library, AA; **40** General Post Office, AA/S Day; **40/41** Cuchuliann Statue, AA/S Day; **42/43** Guinness Storehouse, AA/S Day; **44** Joyce Centre, AA/S Day; **44/45** Joyce Centre, AA/S Day; **45** Joyce Centre, AA/S Day; **46** Kilmainham Gaol, AA/S McBride; **46/47,** Kilmainham Jail, AA/S Whitehorne; **48/49,** National Gallery, AA/Slide File; **50** National Museum of Ireland, AA/S Whitehorne; **50/51** National Museum, AA/S Day; **52** St Patrick's Cathedral, AA/S Whitehorne; **53t** St Patrick's Cathedral, int AA/S Day; **53b** Jonathan Swift Death Mask, AA/S Day; **54** Trinity College, AA/L Blake; **54/55** Trinity College Library, AA/S McBride; **56/57** Howth Head, AA/M Short; **58** Bewley's Oriental Café, AA/M Short; **61** The Oliver St John Gogarty, AA/S Day; **62** Children of Lir Statue, AA/Slide File; **65** Ghost Tour Bus, AA/S Day; **66/67** Smithfield, AA/S Day; **69** Fitzsimon's Inn, AA S/Day; **70** Brooks and Co Antique Shop, AA/W Voysey; **72/73** Four Courts, AA/S Day; **74** The Curragh, AA/S McBride; **75** St Stephen's Green, AA/S Whitehorne; **76/77** Dublin Zoo, AA/M Short; **78/79** O'Shea's Merchant Pub, AA/M Short; **81** Sunlight Chambers, AA/Slide File; **82/83** City Hall Dome, AA/S Day; **84/85** Ha'penny Bridge, AA/S Whitehorne; **86** Dublin Royal Hospital Museum, AA/M Short; **87** Marsh's Library, AA/S Day; **88** St Auden's Church, AA/Slide File; **89** Shaw Birthplace, AA/S Day; **90** Crown Alley, Temple Bar, AA/S Whitehorne; **91** Stained-glass window, Temple Bar pub, AA/S McBride; **92/93** Whitefriars Carmelite Church, AA/S Whitehorne; **95** St Audoen's Arch, AA/S Day; **103** St Stephen's Green, AA/S Day; **104/105** Bank of Ireland, AA; **106** Fitzwilliam Square, AA/Slide File; **106/107** Grafton Street, AA/S Day; **108** Grand Canal, AA/S Whitehorne; **109** Iveagh Gardens, AA/S Day; **111** Stag's Head Pub, AA/S McBride; **112** Merrion Square North, AA/M Short; **113** Leinster House, AA/Slide File; **114/115** National Library Reading Room, AA/S Whitehorne; **116** Natural History Museum, AA/M Short; **116/117** Newman's House, AA/S Whitehorne; **118** Royal College of Surgeons, AA/S Day; **118/119** Oscar Wilde's House, AA/S Day; **119** St Ann's Church, AA/S Day; **120/121** St Stephen's Green, AA/S Day; **133** Moore Street Market, AA/S Day; **134** Abbey Theatre, AA/S Day; **134/135** Blessington Street Basin, AA/S Day; **136** Casino at Marino, AA/S Whitehorne; **136/137** National Museum Collins Barracks, AA/S Day; **138** Custom House, AA/S Day; **138/139** Custom House, AA/S Whitehorne; **139** Dublin Writer's Museum, AA/M Short; **140/141** Phoenix Park Zoological Gardens, AA/S Whitehorne; **141** Four Courts, AA/S Whitehorne; **142/143** O'Connell Monument, AA/S Day; **144** James Joyce Statue, AA; **146/147** Botanic Gardens Palm House, AA/Slide File; **148** Old Jameson Distillery, AA/S Day; **148/149** Phoenix Column, AA/S Day, **150/151** St Michan's Church crypt, AA/Slide File; **151** Smithfield, AA/S Day; **156/157** Malahide Castle, AA/Slide File; **159t** Avoca, AA/M Short; **159b** Cows at Bective Abbey, AA/C Jones; **160** Claremont Landscapes Gardens, AA/D Forss; **160/161** Bray Head, AA/M Short; **162/163** b/g Newgrange, AA/M Short; **163c** Knowth Burial Mound, AA/C Jones; **163b** Bru na Boinne, AA/C Jones; **165** Dalkey, AA/G Munday; **166/167** Magdelaine Tower Drogheda, AA/C Jones; **167** Mural Drogheda, AA/P Zoeller; **168** Trafalgar Square Dun Laoghaire, AA/M Short; **168/169** Glendalough, AA/C Jones; **170/171** Hill of Tara, AA/S Day; **171** Howth, AA/M Short; **172/173** John Oxx Stables Kildare, AA/S McBride; **173** Irish National Stud and Japanese Gardens Kildare, AA/S McBride; **174/175** Killiney Bay, AA/S Whitehorne; **175** Monasterboice, AA/M Short; **176/177** Powerscourt Gardens, AA/M Short; **178** Slane Castle, AA/P Zoeller; **179** Trim, AA/C Jones; **180** Poulaphoca Reservoir, AA/M Short.

Every effort has been made to trace the copyright holders, and we apologise in advance for any unintentional omissions or errors. We would be pleased to apply any corrections in any following edition of this publication.

Street Index